CANADIAN PORTRAITS

EDITED BY NORMAN SHEFFE
Consultant for the Social Sciences
Lincoln County Board of Education
St. Catharines, Ontario

McGRAW-HILL RYERSON LIMITED
Toronto   Montreal   New York   London   Sydney
Johannesburg   Mexico   Panama   Düsseldorf
Singapore   Rio de Janeiro   Kuala Lumpur   New Delhi

CANADIAN PORTRAITS

Sir Isaac Brock, by T. G. Marquis
    Copyright, Canada, by The Ryerson Press, Toronto, 1929.
John Strachan, by W. Stewart Wallace
    Copyright, Canada, by The Ryerson Press, Toronto, 1930.
Lord Selkirk, by W. Martin
    Copyright, Canada, by The Ryerson Press, Toronto, 1926.
Samuel Cunard, by Archibald MacMechan, Ph.D., LL.D.
    Copyright, Canada, by The Ryerson Press, Toronto, 1928.
Sir Sandford Fleming, by Lawrence J. Burpee
    Copyright, Canada, by The Ryerson Press, Toronto, 1930.
Lord Strathcona, by Howard Angus Kennedy
    Copyright, Canada, by The Ryerson Press, Toronto, 1929.

Every effort has been made to locate the authors of these biographies, or their heirs. The publishers would be grateful for any information concerning their whereabouts.

ISBN 0-07-077379-3

1 2 3 4 5 6 7 8 9   HR72   10 9 8 7 6 5 4 3 2

Printed and bound in Canada

CONTENTS

Foreword by the Editor   v

Sir Isaac Brock, by T. G. Marquis   1

John Strachan, by W. Stewart Wallace   33

Lord Selkirk, by W. Martin   63

Samuel Cunard, by
    Archibald MacMechan, Ph.D., LL.D.   95

Sir Sandford Fleming,
    by Lawrence J. Burpee   123

Lord Strathcona,
    by Howard Angus Kennedy   153

Preface

Some forty years ago, Ryerson Press published a series of books for schools under the general title *Canadian History Readers*. A group of skilful, dependable writers turned out approximately one hundred booklets on a wide variety of historical themes. An endorsement from both the Ontario Department of Education and the Imperial Order Daughters of the Empire appeared on the covers. The entire range of the selection of figures reflected a commonly held view of our Canadian past. Many of the writers who contributed to the series went on to achieve prominence in Canadian life. At least one, Rogers, became a cabinet minister; another, W. Stewart Wallace, served as librarian of the largest university in this country; and a third, Lawrence J. Burpee, achieved eminence as an academic historian.

In reissuing a selection of these booklets in the present form, the Ryerson Educational Division of McGraw-Hill Ryerson wishes to place into the hands of readers, some examples of the kind of writing that captures the spirit of the times and inflames the imagination. It is important, however, to specify some of the problems of editing the materials. It was decided to interfere with the original text as little as possible. The changes that were made were those which would clarify the young person's understanding of the past. Obvious errors of fact were corrected, and biases that are no longer acceptable were deleted. In selecting the six portraits presented in this book, it was decided to include nineteenth-century figures outside the narrow world of politics.

If the bias of the historian writing the piece comes through in either a strongly nationalistic or imperialistic colouring, it is not remarkable. To a degree, the historian reflects the thinking of his times. In the two decades following the First World War, the spirit of the times reflected a more positive attitude towards the Commonwealth than is evident today. The reissue of these sketches thus serves two purposes: it informs us about the figures of the past and the view of those figures as seen in an earlier era of this century.

NORMAN SHEFFE

SIR ISAAC BROCK

by

T. G. Marquis

SIR ISAAC BROCK

ISAAC BROCK was born on the little
island of Guernsey, in the year 1769, the
year in which the great Napoleon and the
equally great Wellington were born. The
Brock family was an old one, being able to
trace its descent from the days of William
the Conqueror. It had produced many
military and naval heroes, and stories of
their daring deeds no doubt thrilled young
Isaac Brock, who as a child looked forward
to entering the English army. The lads of
Guernsey were hardy and daring, and
Brock was one of the sturdiest of them. He
was a famous boy boxer and was the best
swimmer among the lads of his time. He
loved reading and delighted in books deal-
ing with great battles and great soldiers.

Brock began his military career at a very
early age. When he was sixteen he joined
the 8th, the King's Regiment, as an ensign.
For three years he was quartered in different parts of England. He was ambitious
to rise in his profession and knew that this
could only be done by study, and so he
spent his leisure morning hours with his

books, locking his door or "sporting his oak," as he no doubt called it, to keep out other young officers. In 1790, he purchased his lieutenancy and was quartered in Guernsey and Jersey. But he did not like soldiering at home, and so, to see service abroad, he got exchanged into the 49th Regiment and joined it in the Barbados. The climate was trying, even to a man as strong as he was, and in 1793, fever almost ended his career; but the devotion of his faithful servant, Dobson, saved his life. Until Dobson's death, shortly before the Battle of Queenston Heights, Brock treated him more like an elder brother than a servant.

In 1797, when twenty-eight years old, Brock became Lieutenant-Colonel of the 49th. It was a time when many officers were brutal to their men. The soldiers of the 49th had been cruelly punished for the slightest offences and when Brock took over the regiment it was in a rebellious spirit—in fact, on the verge of mutiny. Under his kindly leadership a rapid change took place, and soon the 49th, from one of the worst, became known as one of the best regiments in the service.

BROCK DIRECTS THE LANDING OF HIS FORCE ON THE AMERICAN
SHORE FOR THE ATTACK ON DETROIT

Russia and England had formed an alliance against Napoleon, who was trying to bring all Europe under his control, and in 1799, Brock, with the 49th, was sent to Holland to fight under the command of General Sir Ralph Abercrombie. At Egmont-op-Zee the allies and the French fought a fierce battle, and in this fight Brock received his baptism of fire. He had been a soldier for fifteen years, but this was the first time he was under fire. His first battle came near to being his last. In the thick of the fight he was struck with a bullet which tore through his scarf and cravat, slightly wounded him, and knocked him from his horse. But he quickly remounted and gallantly led his men till the end of the action.

After this engagement Brock returned to England, and was for a time once more quartered in Guernsey. The Napoleonic wars were still devastating Europe. Russia had now joined forces with Napoleon and the danger to England was great. An expedition was fitted out, under Sir Hyde Parker and Nelson, to attack the combined Danish and Russian fleets in the Baltic. Brock, who was placed in command of the land forces, was on the *Ganges* during the Battle of Copenhagen, and was near Nelson when he penned his famous message to the Crown Prince of Denmark, a message in many ways like the one afterwards sent by Brock to Hull in Detroit. In the Battle of Copenhagen Admiral Parker, despairing of victory, flew the signal No. 39, to leave off action. Nelson did not heed it, but kept his signal for close action flying. In grim humour he turned to Captain Foley, saying: "You know, Foley, I have only one eye. I have a right to be blind sometimes." And then, putting the glass to his blind eye, he said: "I really do not see the signal," and the fight went on and a glorious victory was won for England.

Brock was a military leader of the Nelson type, and when, later, his commander-in-chief, Prevost, ordered him to do nothing to anger the people of the United States by offensive action, he did not read the words aright, but, contrary to instructions, invaded American territory, won a great victory and saved Canada.

In 1802, the 49th Regiment, with Lieutenant-Colonel Isaac Brock in command,

was sent to Canada, and until Brock's
death ten years later he struggled with
might and main to make his adopted country loyal and a source of strength to Great
Britain in North America. Shortly after
his arrival at Quebec he was sent to Upper
Canada (now Ontario) with headquarters
at York (Toronto).

He was military ruler of the province
and his task was not an easy one. Upper
Canada was largely a wilderness. Roads
were few and bad at that; for the most part
travellers had to resort to blazed trails
through the forests. Ottawa had no existence; Kingston was the chief centre of
population; York was a muddy, unprotected
little village; Hamilton, Amherstburg, Erie,
Queenston, Chippawa, and Fort George
were military stations, but so badly armed
as to be unable to resist an attack of any
strength. The entire population of the province was not much greater than that of the
present city of St. Catharines, Ontario.

The inhabitants were not easy to govern
or control. Land could be had practically
for the asking, and many adventurers from
the United States had flocked in to take up

land and these were having a disloyal effect
on many of the inhabitants and even on
members of the House of Assembly. The
Indians, too, settled principally along the
Grand River, were cause for concern and
Brock feared that, should a war break out,
they would join whatever party proved the
stronger in the first battles. Fortunately,
there were in the province many United
Empire Loyalists, and on these Brock put
great reliance. His soldiers were hard
to manage. Desertions were common and
many selfish soldiers in his force were constantly under temptation from the Americans. Shortly after Brock reached York
seven soldiers deserted, but Brock followed
them at midnight across Lake Ontario, in
an open boat, and captured them near Fort
Niagara on the American shore. A conspiracy, too, was formed at Fort George to
kill the commanding officer, Col. Sheaffe,
and desert in a body to the United States.
Sheaffe was a severe officer and for even
slight offences would inflict the lash on his
soldiers. He was hated with a murderous
hate, and fearing for his life, he sent word
of the conspiracy to Brock, who at once

went to Fort George and arrested the chief conspirators. Brock was sorry for the men, but the crime could not be overlooked, and some of the poor fellows, after a court-martial at Quebec, where they were sent for trial, suffered death for their acts. Brock felt the disgrace to the men of his old regiment keenly, and personally took command at Fort George. He ruled with a firm and yet gentle hand, and so won the hearts of his men that no more desertions were attempted.

In 1805, Brock went to England for a short holiday. Many of his fellow-officers were winning renown and promotion in Europe, and for a time he longed to take part in some of the great European battles; but bad news came from America. There were war clouds there as well as in Europe, and if war broke out he knew that Canada would be invaded swiftly by the United States armies. His heart was in Canada and he quickly cut short his holiday and took passage for Quebec.

On his arrival circumstances were such that for a time he was acting commander-in-chief of the forces in British North

America, with headquarters at Quebec. He found the garrison in a weak condition and had it greatly strengthened, among other things erecting the famous King's battery, first called Brock's, dominating the river and the opposite shore. In 1810, he went to Upper Canada and was in charge of both civil and military affairs at the time of the outbreak of the war of 1812.

War was declared on June 18, 1812, and, as Brock had expected, western Canada, by way of Detroit and Niagara, was to be first attacked. So confident were the Americans of victory, that Dr. Eustis, Secretary of War, thought they could take Canada without soldiers; they had only to send officers into the provinces and the people would rally round the American standard. Henry Clay, the great Southern orator, declared that the Americans had Canada as much under their control as Great Britain had the ocean. He would "take the whole continent" from the English, "and ask them no favours." Ex-President Jefferson looked upon the campaign merely as a matter of marching through to Quebec, after which the capture of Halifax would be easy.

They were reckoning without Brock. A strong, determined man is often worth more than large armies or well-built fortresses— and so it was to prove.

Provost, the commander-in-chief of the British forces in North America, thought that Quebec was the only spot that could be held against the enemy. England could give little help in either men or money, as she was waging a costly war in Europe against Napoleon. The authorities were anxious to prevent war with the United States, and the one cry of the Secretary of War to the commander of the forces was to do nothing to irritate the Americans and to remain strictly on the defensive.

Upper Canada, which must bear the brunt of the war, was in grave danger. Brock had at his back a Legislative Assembly in which there were several disloyal members, and he found it impossible to pass measures necessary for the safety of the province. He distrusted the Indians and he had but little confidence in the militia. Many of the inhabitants were Americans or American sympathizers and in the vicinity of Detroit the population was largely

French who were lukewarm or worse. But Brock held that "the word 'impossible' should not be found in the soldier's dictionary," and he did not despair for the province. With restless energy he rode hither and thither over the rough roads of the west, inspiring confidence and strengthening the positions that were most likely to be attacked. He received word of the declaration of war even before General Hull, the American commander at Detroit, knew of it, and at once made ready to take the offensive. Prevost had been telling him to remain on the defensive, but Brock knew best how to play the war game. Any boy knows that as a general thing the best defence is attack, that the team that contents itself with forming a wall about its goal is almost sure to suffer defeat. It is only by dashing through the forwards, by smashing into the enemy's defence, that games or battles are won. Brock knew that success depended on immediate action; a victory on either side would mean that the Indians and many of the inhabitants would throw in their lot with the victors.

When Brock learned that war was declared, he sent word to Captain Charles Roberts, in command at Fort St. Joseph on Lake Huron, to seize the American fort on Mackinaw Island. This was directly contrary to orders received from Prevost, but Roberts managed to see a way of obeying the orders sent from Brock, and captured Mackinaw with its rich stores without the loss of a man. This success, as Brock had expected, gave the Western Indians confidence in the might of Great Britain, and kept them faithful allies.

Hull entered Canada on July 12, 1812. He met with a feeble resistance at Sandwich. He had intended to march against the fort at Amherstburg, but delayed until he could go against it with greater force. He contented himself with threatening all sorts of dreadful things to the inhabitants if they opposed his troops, and sending out his soldiers along the river Thames to plunder peaceful farmers and steal sheep, cattle, and provisions.

Brock meanwhile was working hard to get together a force strong enough to attack Hull. At York he issued a call for volunteers and met with great success. The sturdy sons of farmers, the few professional men, and the leading legislators all took up arms, and the mothers of Upper Canada put weapons in their sons' hands and urged them on to the battle. One boy wrote:

"As far as I was myself concerned, had I ever been disposed to hang back it would have been at the risk of suffering the most severe reproaches from my mother—who at parting, as she clasped me in her arms and then tore herself from my embrace, exclaimed: 'Go, my son, and let me hear of your death rather than your disgrace.' I marched off with a full heart and a buoyant spirit."

Brock by this time had so strengthened Fort George that he felt confident of being able to resist any force that might try to cross the Niagara river at that point. He now turned his attention to the Detroit river, and as soon as he had enrolled the volunteers he required he determined to go to that district, draw Hull into a battle, and, if possible, drive him out of Canada; and he even hoped for the capture of Detroit itself.

While he seemed to be sure of success, in his heart he had many doubts. He had not sufficient arms for his men, military clothing was scarce and many of the volunteers were even without shoes. But it was necessary to strike a decisive blow to keep the wavering loyal and to strike terror into the hearts of American sympathizers. He depended mainly on the United Empire Loyalists and their sons. The strong company of volunteers he had enrolled at York, with the few regulars he had at his command, must lead the way.

There were many delays and it was the sixth of August before he was able to set out for Detroit on an expedition that was to turn aside the tide of war for the time being at any rate. The Detroit expedition went first to Burlington Bay and then overland to Lake Erie. When passing the Mohawk settlement on the Grand River, on August 7, Brock held a council of war for finding out the spirit of the Indians. He found them lukewarm; Hull's agents had been among them and Brock received only a half-hearted promise that sixty warriors would follow after him. He feared that, if his expedition failed, the Indians, for whom England had done so much, might be counted as enemies.

On August 8, Brock reached Long Point on Lake Erie, where open boats were in readiness to convey the troops up the lake. It was a time of storm; strong winds buffeted them, rain descended almost continuously, and four days passed before the force reached Amherstburg.

On the day of Brock's arrival, Hull, in alarm, withdrew the last of the American troops from Sandwich, which was at once occupied by a British force, and in two days' time five guns bearing on Fort Detroit were in position.

Shortly after his arrival at the Detroit river Brock learned through the capture of an American force by the great Indian chief, Tecumseh, that letters sent out by Hull showed that the American general was in no happy frame of mind. His supplies were running short, there was much sickness among his troops, and he was so far from a base of supplies that he felt he could not stand a long siege, should Brock attempt to capture Detroit. He was no longer thinking of making a triumphal march through Canada. When Brock read Hull's letters he at once decided on a daring course; he would attack Hull in his strongly fortified position. He knew that Hull had under his command a fighting force of about 2,500 men—double the number he could muster. He expected no easy or bloodless victory, but thought he would try negotiations before making an attack and sent the following message to Hull:

"The force at my disposal authorizes me to require of you the immediate surrender of Fort Detroit. It is far from my inclination to join in a war of extermination; but you must be aware that the numerous body of Indians who have attached themselves to my troops will be beyond my control the moment the contest commences. You will find me disposed to enter into such conditions as will satisfy the most scrupulous sense of honour. . . ."

Brock was profiting by the lesson he had learned from Nelson at Copenhagen, and putting on a bold front, strengthened his demand for surrender with an implied threat. His bluff did not have immediate

success. Hull would no doubt have surrendered gladly, but he had to make some
show of defence, and so he replied that he
was ready to meet any force which might
be at Brock's disposal. The Sandwich bat-
teries then opened fire and the fort replied,
but as little damage was done on either side
Brock gave orders to cease firing. He then
decided to cross the river in force. In this
decision he was strongly supported by
Tecumseh, who, to aid him in his undertaking, spread a piece of birch-bark on the
ground and with a hunting-knife traced on
it an excellent military map of the American
shore, showing the streams to be crossed,
the groves where shelter might be taken and
the approaches to Fort Detroit. Brock now
decided to cross the river on the morning of
the 16th, and if possible draw Hull into
battle.

The troops slept with their weapons be-
side them, and as the first flush of dawn
stole grey and cool over the summer morning, made preparations for the crossing.
Canoes and boats of every kind were col-
lected, and in them 330 regulars and 400
militia were embarked, with five pieces of

artillery. A landing was made four or five miles below Detroit, and no attempt was made to oppose it. During the night 600 Indians, under Colonel Elliott and Tecumseh, had crossed to attack the Americans in front and rear, if any attempt were made to drive back Brock's little army.

Brock had fewer than 1,400 men with whom to do battle against a force of over 2,500; these, too, were in a strong fortress armed with heavy cannon and had plenty of ammunition. On the face of it, the invasion was one of the most daring ever attempted in war. But Brock knew the man opposed to him and was confident that Hull would be easily defeated if he could be made to come out of his fort and fight. When he reached the American shore he decided on an even bolder plan. He would not wait for Hull to come against him, but he would try to capture the fort itself. He learned that a body of between 300 and 400 troops were absent from the garrison, trying to bring in much-needed supplies. They were on the homeward march, so Brock boldly advanced his men against the fortress in the hope that he could cause its fall before these troops arrived to greatly strengthen Hull.

The fort Brock was attempting to capture, with his 600 Indians and 700 regulars and militia, was of great strength. It was built in the form of a parallelogram, with strong bastions at the corners, and had a moat, or ditch, eight feet deep and twelve feet wide, surrounding it. About it was a palisade of hardwood stakes. The rampart rose perpendicularly twenty-two feet and was pierced with embrasures for cannon. It had a portcullis, well-ironed, on the east front, protected by a projecting framework of huge logs standing over the moat and pierced for small arms. It had a drawbridge and sallyports near the southern and northern bastions. It had abundant stores of ammunition, over thirty guns ranging from 24-pounders down, and, best of all, to the south for two miles there were no obstructions and to the west for a mile and a half a level common. The force under Hull was so arranged that it could mass swiftly at any point where invaders might show themselves. The very road along which Brock had chosen to advance was guarded by two 24-pounders. All the guns were loaded and ready for action.

The British troops boldly advanced until within range of the guns, while the battery at Sandwich and the guns on a vessel, the *Queen Charlotte*, opened on the fort, one shot bursting within the walls and killing a number of American soldiers. The Indians meanwhile were advancing with warlike yells. The soldiers in the fort stood with lighted matches by the loaded guns, but Hull gave no command to begin action. The 24-pounders guarding the road over which Brock was advancing were abandoned and the soldiers fled to the shelter of the fort. They brought such an exaggerated account of the number of the enemy to Hull, who was in a safe retreat behind a heavy beam, that he was led to believe he had several thousand regulars to contend with. The blood-curdling yells of the Indians, too, did much to increase his fears, and, believing that a vast host of them had joined the British, he decided to surrender and sent out an aide-de-camp with a flag of truce.

Brock was much surprised at Hull's act, but he was greatly pleased. He could ill afford to lose men and he had been expecting that cannon ball and shell would shortly be ploughing their way through his troops. This white flag seemed too good to be true; but it was a fact and Hull and his force, double that of the British, tamely surrendered forty cannon, 3,000 muskets, a vast supply of musket cartridges, sixty barrels of gunpowder, 180 tons of lead, and 200 tons of cannon ball, while much food fell into the hands of the conquerors.

There was great rejoicing in Canada when news of this astonishing victory was received and, later, even greater rejoicing in England. British soldiers and British ships had been suffering losses in battle and the fall of Detroit was the first cause for rejoicing the English people had had in many months. The guns of the Tower of London thundered out news of the victory, and the King of England made the victor an extra Knight of the Order of the Bath.

On the day that the Tower guns told England that Detroit had fallen, Brock's brother, with his wife, was walking in a

London park. The wife asked the cause of
the salute. "Don't you know," her husband replied jokingly, "this is Isaac's birthday; it is in honour of him." When they
returned home they learned that in very
truth the guns had been fired in honour of
their brave brother.

Hull had intended to march at his leisure
to Quebec. He was not to be disappointed,
only he went there, with all his regular
troops, under a strong guard. The victory
had the effect of striking terror into the
hearts of the untrained American soldiers
and of giving hope to all Canadians. The
sight of the prisoners as they marched
through Canada—stopping at York, Kingston, Montreal, and finally Quebec—taught
the people that they need not despair; that
in Brock they had a tower of strength
guarding their borders.

Now followed an action that completely
overthrew the plans of Brock. As soon as
he had finished settling affairs at Detroit,
he set sail down Lake Erie with the intention of sweeping the Americans from the
Niagara frontier. But he was met by a
vessel bearing the news that an armistice had

been agreed upon between the commanders-in-chief of the opposing forces, Generals Prevost and Dearborn, and that all warfare must end.

The Americans made good use of the armistice. The Niagara frontier was weakly held and in the lull in warfare they put forth all their energies to rush supplies and men into the region lying between Lake Ontario and Lake Erie. Brock could make no such use of the lull in warfare, as he had neither extra supplies nor men to draw upon. After Detroit, by swift action, he could have driven the enemy from the Niagara frontier and destroyed or held their strongholds. When the armistice came to an end, he found opposed to him an army four times larger than his own, cannon stationed at every important point, and huge supplies piled up for the support of the American army.

Brock was glad when the armistice came to an end. He could not now hope to invade American territory, but even with his absurdly small army he made plans to keep the enemy out of Canada. He had been two months in the field and yet, in his own words, "not a single death, either natural or by the sword," had happened among his men, and—a thing that gave him great pride—no soldier had deserted.

It was expected that the Americans, who had some 6,300 men along the river between Fort Niagara and Black Rock, would attempt to invade Canadian territory, feeling sure that they could brush aside Brock's small force of 1,500 men. Between October 9 and 13, preparations had on several occasions been made to cross the river at Queenston, but nothing of a serious nature happened until the early morning of October 13.

Brock had been unceasingly watchful, and news of the intentions of the enemy had come to him. On the 12th of October he was at Fort George, planning how best to keep the Americans from getting a foothold on Canadian soil. From reports he had received he thought that they would make an attack in force at Fort George, but he also feared that they might attempt to cross the river at Queenston. With his small force, and the feeble support he had from the Government, he feared for Upper Canada,

BROCK'S RIDE TO QUEENSTON

and the night before the Battle of Queenston Heights, he wrote a letter to one of his brothers, in which he said: "If I should be beaten, the province is inevitably gone." He then went to rest fully expecting battle on the morrow.

Long before daylight the distant roar of guns told a watchful sentry at Fort George that the Americans had begun firing on Queenston. He promptly brought the news to Brock, who, calling for his good horse, Alfred, speedily dressed, and was soon galloping along the road leading to Queenston Heights. The roar of the cannon grew louder as he advanced, and he put spurs to his horse. The morning was cold, a drizzling rain was falling, but he bent to the storm and strained every nerve to reach the scene of battle. As he galloped through the darkness, a horseman approached at full speed. It was Lieutenant Jarvis, who had been sent to Brock with news that the Americans were attempting an invasion in full force. So swiftly was Jarvis approaching that he could not rein up his horse, nor did Brock pause; he merely turned in his saddle and waved his hand to Jarvis to follow after him. They were soon galloping side by side and when Brock got details of the attempted invasion, he knew that there was no danger at Fort George, and that he must pay all his attention to Queenston Heights. Without pausing, he told Jarvis to speed at once to Fort George and tell General Sheaffe, whom he had left in command there, to hasten to Queenston with every man that could be spared from the garrison and at the same time to have the Indians, many of whom were encamped at Fort George, advance through the woods on the right to protect Sheaffe's men from surprise.

Brock soon reached Brown's Point, three miles from the scene of battle. Here he received a rousing cheer from the company stationed there, the York Volunteers under Captain Cameron. Ordering Cameron to follow after him with the York volunteers as quickly as he could, he once more put spurs to his horse. At Vrooman's Point, a mile or so from Queenston Heights, there was a 24-pounder gun and a small body of men under Captain Howard. He briefly inspected the post, gave a word of praise to

Howard's men for the good work they were doing, and once more took up his wild gallop to the scene of battle.

The fight had now been raging since three o'clock in the morning. Thirteen boats, heavily loaded with men, had attempted to cross the swiftly flowing Niagara river. At first they tried to steal across with muffled oars, but a sentry saw them while they were still in mid-stream and volley after volley was poured into the crowded boats. The American leader, Colonel Van Rensselaer, was severely wounded, several of the boats met disaster and the troops in them were captured; only a few succeeded in landing and these had to take shelter along the steep bank of the river. The guns on the American shore were in readiness to protect the landing and so soon as the crossing boats were attacked, two 18-pounders, two mortars and two 6-pounders above the village of Lewiston began thundering against Queenston. The Canadian gunners were not idle and the guns in the village of Queenston and along the Canadian shore and the one gun stationed on

Queenston Heights poured shot and shell into the advancing boats.

Brock, as soon as he arrived at Queenston, went up the hill to the single gun to get a good view of the whole scene of action. From this point he saw strong bodies of American soldiers waiting to cross the river; but he saw, too, that his artillery and infantry officers were beating back the attempts of the enemy to land on the Canadian shore. He thought there was no danger from the Heights, and so he sent Captain Williams, with the light company guarding this point, down to the village of Queenston to help in the battle there. It was a fatal mistake. He was left with but eight artillerymen at the gun. As he continued to examine the action, to his surprise a body of men appeared on the summit of the hill. They were some sixty American soldiers, who, under Captain Wool, had scaled a difficult path and now had the crew of the gun at their mercy. A hail of bullets fell about them and Brock and his eight men made a hurried retreat to Queenston village.

A British soldier feels nothing more keenly than the loss of a gun, and Brock at once determined to personally lead a force to recapture the battery on the heights and if possible capture the Americans or drive them back to their own shore. There was no immediate danger at the village, and so, gathering together two companies of the 49th Regiment and one hundred militia, he set out on his dangerous task. "Follow me, boys!" he shouted cheerily, as he led off his men at a brisk trot. At the base of the hill he halted to give his men a brief rest before ordering them to charge up the slope. He here dismounted, climbed over a high stone wall, and, drawing his sword, gallantly led his men against the enemy.

By this time Captain Wool had a force of fully 400 soldiers under his command. Under the circumstances it was almost foolhardy to attempt the recapture of the gun. But Brock was a fearless soldier, and every man at his back was ready to follow his leader to victory or death. Brock, over six feet tall, in full regimentals, waving his sword as he advanced, was an easy mark for the enemy. As he drew close to the enemy, one of them stepped deliberately in front of his fellows, took steady aim and shot down the British commander. It was a fatal shot, and without uttering a word Brock fell dead with his face to the foe. His men kept up the fight a few moments longer, but the firing was so severe that they were forced to retreat.

They succeeded in carrying the body of their leader back with them to Queenston, where it rested for the remainder of that day of battle. The news of his death was a terrible blow to his men, but they were not disheartened. His spirit animated them all, and their battle cry now was: "Avenge the General!" From Fort George and Chippawa troops were coming. Before evening the force on the hill was hemmed in and a complete victory won by the British.

. Brock was dead, but Canada was saved. Had the Americans succeeded in landing in force at Queenston, the whole province of Upper Canada would have been in their hands before snow fell. For his noble work and his heroic death Brock has been and will ever be known as

THE HERO OF UPPER CANADA

BISHOP JOHN STRACHAN

by

W. Stewart Wallace

JOHN STRACHAN

O N THE last day of the eighteenth century, December 31, 1799, there arrived in the town of Kingston, in Upper Canada, a young Scots schoolmaster, of twenty-one years of age, named John Strachan. Kingston, though at that time the largest town in Upper Canada, was still little more than a backwoods village, having been founded only sixteen years before by the United Empire Loyalists who had come to the shores of the Bay of Quinté to carve for themselves homes from the forest primeval. It was a town of less than two hundred houses, most of them built of logs; it had only one church, which resembled a barn rather than a church; and it had no public buildings except the barracks of the tiny British garrison. It had no newspaper and no library.

Such was the new home in which John Strachan, a graduate of Aberdeen University, found himself. He was welcomed as a tutor in the house of the leading merchant in Kingston, the Honourable Richard Cartwright, a member of the Legislative Council of Upper Canada; and here he was made as comfortable as circumstances would permit.

Yet it must have been with a sinking of the heart that he surveyed his primitive surroundings—surroundings, no doubt, very different from those which he had pictured in imagination on his long journey from his native land. Nor is it likely that he—or, indeed, any one else—had any idea that his arrival in Kingston was an event of much moment. If any one in Kingston had been told that the appearance of the young schoolmaster was fraught with profound importance for the future history of Upper Canada, he would have found it difficult to credit the prophecy. Yet such a prophecy would have been not short of the truth; for John Strachan was destined to exert on the affairs of his adopted country during the next half century or more an influence perhaps as great as that of any one else.

The new-comer was not a young man of patrician birth. He had not been born with a silver spoon in his mouth. His father had been an overseer in an Aberdeenshire stone-quarry, who had been killed by a blast at the quarry when John Strachan was only fourteen years of age. Since the death of his father, John Strachan had become the chief support of his widowed mother; and for

JOHN STRACHAN, FIRST BISHOP OF TORONTO, AND THE BEAUTIFUL
GOTHIC GATE AND DOORWAY OF ST. JAMES' CATHEDRAL, TORONTO.
BISHOP STRACHAN LAID THE CORNERSTONE IN 1850, AND DEDI-
CATED THE EDIFICE IN 1853. THE BISHOP HAD HIS CHAIR IN ST.
JAMES', AS HAVE HIS SUCCESSORS.

many years after he came to Canada he continued to send home a monthly remittance.
By means familiar to many a Scottish under-
graduate of that and later times, he worked
his way through Aberdeen University; and
thus he entered himself as a divinity student
at the University of St. Andrews, earning a
livelihood meanwhile as a parish school-
teacher. Among his pupils was at least one
who later became famous, the painter Sir
David Wilkie.

At St. Andrew's Strachan made the ac-
quaintance of a certain Thomas Chalmers,
who was later to become a notable figure in
Scottish ecclesiastical history as the leader
of the disruption that led to the formation of
the Free Church of Scotland in 1843; and
it was through Chalmers that Strachan obtained the opening that brought him to
Upper Canada. The first lieutenant-governor of Upper Canada, Colonel John
Graves Simcoe, had had the idea of founding
in the province a college or university. The
idea was premature, and Simcoe left the
province, in 1796, without having made any
progress with the project. But, in 1798, the
step was taken of setting aside a large sec-
tion of the Crown lands of the province, to

be used as an endowment for educational purposes; and the plan was formed by some of the leading men in the colony of establishing a school which might later develop into a college or university. The headmastership of this school was offered to Thomas Chalmers. Had Chalmers accepted it, one cannot help reflecting, the history of both Canada and Scotland might have been very different; on such apparently trivial decisions does history sometimes turn. But Chalmers, for reasons which can only be surmised, declined the offer, and recommended Strachan in his place. Strachan, then barely of age, was attracted by the position, since it seemed to offer better prospects than anything he had in view in Scotland; and in the autumn of 1799 he sailed for Canada.

Great was his disappointment when he arrived at his destination. In Kingston he found that the project of a school or college had fallen through, and that the only post awaiting him was that of tutor to the children of Richard Cartwright and two or three other of the more affluent inhabitants of the town. "I was so beat down," he wrote later, "that, if I had been in possession of twenty pounds, I should have returned at once; but in truth I had not twenty shillings, and was therefore obliged to make the best of it." In what manner he succeeded in making "the best of it" will appear as this narrative progresses. For three years he conducted at Kingston, in the home of Richard Cartwright, a small private school; and one must regard his pupils as singularly fortunate in having such a tutor, for most of the school teachers in Upper Canada at that time were discharged soldiers whose chief qualification for instructing the young was the fact that they were incapacitated for manual labour. But Strachan had not come to Canada to be a tutor in a gentleman's family; and his thoughts turned again to the Church as a means of preferment. In 1802 he applied for the position of minister of the Scots Presbyterian Church in Montreal, but he was too late in his application; and the following year he applied for, and obtained, the appointment as rector of the Church of England at Cornwall, Upper Canada. In the spring of 1803 he was ordained, by the Anglican bishop of Quebec, a clergyman of the Church of England.

This ordination had far-reaching results.

In after years, John Strachan became an uncompromising protagonist of the exclusive claims of the Church of England in Canada, even against the claims of the Church of Scotland. This was an evidence of his thorough-going nature; for he was like Thomas à Becket, who, while he was the king's man, was a devoted servant of the king, but who, when he became the Pope's man, was an equally devoted servant of the Pope. But his rather easy change of religious affiliation greatly intensified feeling against him later among large elements of the people of Upper Canada; and the agitator Robert Gourlay went so far as to describe him as "a lying little fool of a renegade Presbyterian." There was, in truth, nothing very unusual in 1803 in Strachan's change from the Church of Scotland to that of England; for religious lines among Protestants were not at that time rigidly drawn. But many people failed to understand Strachan's later opposition to the claims of the Church to which he had once belonged, and were apt to regard him with antagonism.

The stipend of the rector of Cornwall was by no means princely. Strachan was still in the position of having to send money back to his widowed mother in Scotland; and in order to add to his income he opened a school at Cornwall. He was a born schoolmaster; and a description of his method of teaching arithmetic, which he has left us in the preface to *A Concise Introduction to Practical Arithmetic*, published by him in Montreal in 1809, illustrates his thoroughness and efficiency:

I beg leave to notice my method of teaching Arithmetic, as it may be of use to those teachers who have not yet acquired much experience. In a new country like this a variety of branches must be taught in every respectable school. Young men coming from a distance at a very considerable expense are anxious to get forward as fast as possible, and even those destined for the learned professions are seldom allowed the time requisite for acquiring the knowledge previously necessary. These considerations induced me to turn my thoughts to the Discovery of some sure and at the same time expeditious method of teaching Arithmetic. This object I have accomplished with a much greater degree of success than I dared to promise

myself . . . Each class have one or
more sums to produce every day, neatly
wrought upon their slates. The work is
carefully examined, after which I command every figure to be blotted out and the
sums to be wrought under my eye. The
one whom I happen to pitch upon first
gives, with an audible voice, the rules and
reasons for every step, and as he proceeds
the rest silently work along with him,
figure for figure, but ready to correct him
if he blunder, that they may get his place.
As soon as this one is finished, the work
is again blotted out and another called
upon to work the question aloud as before,
while the rest again proceed along with
him in silence, and so on round the whole
class. By this method the principles are
fixed in the mind, and he must be a very
dull boy indeed who does not understand
every question thoroughly before he leave
it. This method of teaching Arithmetic
possesses the important advantage that it
may be pursued without interrupting the
Pupil's progress in any other useful
study. The same method of teaching
Algebra has been used with equal
success. Such a plan is certainly very

laborious, but it will be found successful, and he that is anxious to spare labour ought not to be a Public teacher . . . .

One of his pupils, George Ridout, in a letter written to his father, in 1807, has given us a vivid picture of Strachan and of his school at work:

Mr. Strachan is building a new school-house, about forty feet by thirty. It is to be arched, and there are twelve windows in it. In the meantime he keeps school in the church. I am now in the surveying class, and Mr. Strachan gives us a figure to work every night. We have made ourselves quadrants out of cherry-wood, which cost us two shillings to be made smooth, and we are now in Euclid, 6th book, which is the furthest Mr. Strachan teaches his boys. He knows to the 12th. We are now making preparations for the examination, which will be five weeks from to-day. Some have to make their own speeches, and I among the number. The question is, Whether general History or Biography is the most useful? Mr. Strachan has now been married nearly two months, he lives in great style, and

keeps three servants. He is a great friend
to the poor, and spends his money as fast
as he gets it. He is very passionate.

It was not long before the Cornwall school
had built up for itself a reputation as the best
in the province. It attracted to it the sons of
the leading families as far away as York
(Toronto), the infant capital of the province; and thus the schoolmaster was brought
into touch with the governing class in the
colony—the families which at a later date
came to be known, rather unfairly, as the
"Family Compact." Not all of Strachan's
pupils, however, were the sons of influential
people. His most distinguished pupil, Sir
John Beverley Robinson, came to him as the
penniless son of a widow, and was educated
by him *gratis*. If he owed something to the
Family Compact, the Family Compact owed
not a little to him.

Up to this point Strachan had been a poor
man, with no prospects outside the Church
and school-teaching. In 1807, however, he
married the widow of Andrew McGill, the
brother of that James McGill who founded
McGill University. Andrew McGill had
been what was, for those days, a rich man;

and his widow brought to her second husband a "comfortable annuity," which relieved him of financial embarrassment. There is an interesting story told of this marriage, which may or may not be true. It is said that Mrs. McGill, who was before her first marriage a Miss Wood of Cornwall, had been engaged originally to Strachan, and that Andrew McGill had proposed marriage to her after Strachan and she had become affianced. With the old-fashioned sense of honour prevalent in those days, and knowing that Strachan was not yet in a position to support her, she had come to him and asked him what she should do, telling him at the same time that Andrew McGill, who was by no means a young man, had promised to leave her his fortune on his death. The story is that Strachan, in his broad Scots accent, said, "Tak' him." She took him, and two or three years later he died. Then Strachan reaped the reward of his prudence and patience, and they were married.

Whatever the truth of this story, which is based only on tradition, but is not otherwise incredible, there is no doubt that Strachan's marriage was a turning-point in his career. His wife was not only a woman of excellent qualities, but her money enabled him to devote himself more freely to the pursuit of his ideals and ambitions. He had many interests; but his interest in education was a golden thread which shot through the whole of his career from early youth to aged death. It was significant that, in the very year of his marriage, he was influential in obtaining the passage of an Act which, for the first time, established a system of public "grammar schools" (as they were called) in Upper Canada. He made the mistake of linking these grammar schools too closely with the Church of England; and this mistake had later to be undone. But he deserves the credit of being, in some degree, the father of state-supported schools in the province of Upper Canada or Ontario.

In 1811 he was honoured by his Alma Mater, the University of Aberdeen, with the degree of doctor of divinity; and in 1812 he was appointed rector of York, the capital of Upper Canada. There is reason to believe that he would have preferred the rectorship of Kingston, which had fallen vacant the year before on the death of his spiritual adviser, the Rev. John Stuart. Stuart, like Strachan, had been originally a Presby-

terian; and between the two men there had
been a close bond of sympathy. But Mrs.
Stuart, the widow of the rector at Kingston,
had desired that her son, the Rev. George
O'Kill Stuart, should succeed his father;
and Strachan took the living which the Rev.
George O'Kill Stuart had resigned, the rectorship of York. The result was fortunate.
Strachan's appointment to York brought him
into closer touch with those who governed
the province, and almost immediately his
native ability and strength of character
brought him to the fore. Hardly had he been
appointed rector of York when the War of
1812 broke out; and in this struggle he had
an opportunity of revealing the stuff of
which he was made.

Not being a combatant (and there were no
regimental chaplains in those days),
Strachan took no direct part in the events of
1812; but the occupation of York by the
Americans under General Dearborn, in the
last week of April, 1813, brought him
into the limelight. The British General
Sheaffe, before evacuating the town, left
Colonel Chewett of the York Volunteers in
charge, with instructions to capitulate on the
best terms possible. Colonel Chewett, when

the Americans landed, associated with himself Dr. Strachan (as he now was) and John Beverley Robinson, the acting attorney-general of the province. But when difficulties arose in regard to the ratification by General Dearborn of the articles of capitulation, it was Strachan who, alone and at his own request, bearded the American general in his den. We have an account of the interview between the two men; and it must be confessed that Strachan did not come off second best. Dearborn was in a bad temper, and told Strachan that the best thing he could do was to keep out of his (Dearborn's) way, and not follow him, as he had business of much greater importance to attend to. "In fine," reported the deputation, he "treated him with the utmost disrespect." Strachan thereupon turned to Commodore Chauncey, the American naval commander, who was present, and remarked to him that this was "a new way of treating people clothed in a public character." He had had, he said, the honour of transacting business with greater men than General Dearborn without meeting insult. It was easy, he continued, to see through General Dearborn's backwardness in ratifying the capitulation. While the terms of surrender were unsigned, the American soldiers were plundering the town; and no doubt General Dearborn was reluctant to sign the capitulation until the town had been thoroughly plundered, so that he could say that he had protected property—after everything of value had been stolen. Passionately, the doughty clergyman declared he would not be so duped and insulted; and if the terms of surrender were not immediately ratified, the British would not recognize them. The Americans might do their worst; but they would not have it in their power to say that they had respected private property after the town had been looted.

This courageous stand of the rector of York produced its result. Dearborn— whose rudeness had been so adroitly rebuked by Strachan through words addressed, not to him, but to his fairer-minded naval colleague—shortly afterwards agreed to sign the capitulation; and the depredations of the invaders were thus deprived of any justification. Later, when the behaviour of the American troops gave rise to trouble, Strachan headed a second deputation which waited on General Dearborn, and compelled

the American to make an effort to control his
ill-disciplined troops. Indeed, when he
found two American soldiers engaged in
looting, he promptly intervened; and when
one of the American soldiers levelled his
musket at the intrepid clergyman, only the
arrival of an American officer on the scene
prevented what might have been a serious
contre-temps. No one who examines the
story of that hectic week, during which the
Americans occupied the little capital of
Upper Canada in the spring of 1813, can
fail to realize that there was one man in York
who was worthy of the name, and that his
name was John Strachan.

The part played by Strachan in York during the War of 1812 naturally commended
him to the government of Upper Canada;
and shortly after the conclusion of peace
he was appointed a member of the Executive
Council of the province. He thus became,
in 1815, an important personage in what
came to be known later as the "Family Compact." He was, at this time, only thirty-six
years of age; he was of humble birth; and he
had no influential family connections in the
province at all. That he should, under these
circumstances, have risen to occupy

one of the "seats of the mighty" was not only
an evidence of his character and ability, but
was also a striking commentary on the re-
puted exclusiveness of the "Family
Compact."

From the date of his appointment to the
Executive Council of Upper Canada,
Strachan began to exert a commanding
influence in the affairs of the province. He
built himself in York a residence to which
he gave the name of "The Palace"—a residence so pretentious for those days that
when his brother, James Strachan, came
from Scotland to visit him in 1819, he
ventured the remark, "I hope it's a' come by
honestly, Jock." An increasing number of
the young men who had attended his school
in Cornwall found places in the government
offices; and in 1820, when the lieutenant-
governor of the province, Sir Peregrine Maitland, desired to find "some confidential
person through whom to make communica-
tions" in the Legislative Council of the province, he chose Strachan, who thus became
the special spokesman of the lieutenant-
governor in the Legislative Council, as well
as a member of the Executive Council.
How Sir Peregrine Maitland, a blue-blooded

aristocrat who had commanded the first brigade of the Guards at Waterloo, came to select as his mouthpiece in the Colonial legislature the son of an Aberdeenshire quarryman is not easy of explanation; but apparently the man who had led the Guards in the final charge at Waterloo, when Wellington said, "Up, Guards, and at them," knew a man when he saw him, no matter how strong his Scots accent might be.

For the next twenty years, Strachan became one of the pillars of the "Family Compact." That his influence on the course of events during these years was always beneficial, it would be folly to pretend. He made the fatal mistake of identifying both himself and the "Family Compact" with the exclusive claims of the Church of England in Upper Canada, when he must have known that the adherents of that Church in the province were in a decided minority. The Constitutional Act of 1791 had set apart one-seventh of all lands granted in the province, for the establishment of a "clergy reserve," to be used for "the maintenance and support of a Protestant clergy." Strachan, who regarded the Church of England as the established Church of the province, championed the exclusive claims of this Church to these lands, even to the exclusion of the established Church of Scotland. He also endeavoured to assert the right of the Church of England to control education, both in the grammar schools and in a state-endowed university. In his championship of the claims of the Church of England, he made the deplorable mistake of attempting to cast a slur on the loyalty of the adherents of other denominations, especially of the Methodists, who belonged to "the conference of the United States of America." It is undeniable that the Methodists of Upper Canada were in close affiliation at this time with the Methodists of the United States, and were to some extent influenced by them; but the attempt to call in question the loyalty of the Methodists to the British Crown can only be described as a ghastly *faux pas* on the part of Strachan. Even in political matters, he was not always wise. When, at a later date, William Lyon Mackenzie was making things uncomfortable for the "Family Compact" in the Legislative Assembly, and there was some doubt as to the lawfulness of his proposed expulsion from the Assembly, Strachan was reported to have said, "Never mind the law; toorn him oot."

It is significant that when Sir John Colborne, the sanest of all the lieutenant-governors of Upper Canada, succeeded Sir Peregrine Maitland, in 1828, he wrote of Strachan: "I cannot blind myself so far as not to be convinced that the political part he has taken in Upper Canada destroys his clerical influence, and injures to a very great degree the interests of the Episcopal Church, and, I am afraid, of religion also." Perhaps some consciousness of this fact dawned also on the mind of Strachan himself, for during the régime of Sir John Colborne he withdrew more and more from political life; and, in 1836, he resigned from the Executive Council of the province. Yet he continued to be a member of the Legislative Council of the province until just before the union of Upper and Lower Canada in 1840; and there is no doubt that his advocacy of the exclusive claims of the Church of England to the "clergy reserves" and the control of education was one of the major causes of the rebellion of 1837. Before either the rebellion or the union took place, however, he had ceased to be an active participant in

Upper Canadian politics, and had begun to devote himself to the educational and religious work which lay nearest his heart.

It was in education that he was destined to make his deepest mark in the history of his adopted country. We have seen what a success he made of his school at Cornwall. When he came to York, he took charge of the York Grammar School—familiarly known as "the Old Blue School"—and of this also he made a success. In 1823 he was appointed president of the General Board of Education which was created in that year in Upper Canada, and the following year he was largely responsible for an Act of the legislature which inaugurated a system of financial grants to "common schools," and appointed boards in each district of the province for the examination of teachers. It was he, also, who persuaded Sir Peregrine Maitland to take up, in 1825, the long-deferred project of the establishment of a university in the province—the "university or college" which he had, it will be remembered, come to Canada originally, in 1799, to found. It was he who, in 1826, went to England, and induced the British government to grant a charter for the establishment

of a college, "with the style and privileges of
a university, for the education and instruc-
tion of youth in Arts and Faculties, to continue for ever to be called King's College."
Of this college, which was destined to evolve
into the University of Toronto, he became
the first president.

It is true that his conception of education
was not that which was destined to prevail
in Upper Canada. He regarded education
as the handmaid of religion; and he strove
to bring both the common schools of the province and King's College under the ecclesiastical control of the Church of England. In King's College, for example, all
the members of the College Council were to
subscribe to the Thirty-Nine Articles; and
degrees in divinity were to be restricted to
members of the Church of England. But
the idea that education should not be
divorced from religion is a conception which
is not wholly impossible of defence; and, if
Strachan's ideas of religion were perhaps
too rigorously exclusive, Canada nevertheless owes him a debt of gratitude for the
efforts which he made on behalf of education
when educational facilities in the province
were sadly lacking.

One cannot, moreover, fail to admire his faith in his own ideas and his courage in pursuing them. It took him fifteen years, in the face of the bitterest opposition, to get King's College into operation; and it had been in operation only seven years when it was secularized, and transformed into the "godless" university of Toronto. One might have expected that this defeat of Strachan's ideals would have, after so many years of struggle, dashed his spirits; but it was not so. Though already an old man of over seventy years of age, he set himself to build anew the temple of his dreams. He went to England, and there obtained the funds for the establishment in 1852 of a new university, the University of Trinity College, which should perpetuate his ideal of higher education under the wing of what he regarded as the true Church. It falls to very few men to found, during their lives, two universities; but such was the achievement of John Strachan—and it is worthy of note that he had also a hand in founding McGill University in Montreal, for it was he who suggested to James McGill that he should leave a bequest for this purpose. Whatever one may think of Strachan's educational ideals, one must admit that to his zeal for education Canada owes an undischargeable debt.

Of his ecclesiastical career, little need be said here. He was one of the great figures in the history of the Church of England in Canada. In 1825 he was appointed arch-deacon of York; and in 1839, when Upper Canada was detached from the diocese of Quebec, he became the first Anglican bishop of Toronto. For nearly thirty years he administered with great ability the affairs of the Church of England in Upper Canada; and it was only a few months before his death in 1867—at the age of eighty-nine years—that he consented to the appointment of a coadjutor.

In many ways John Strachan was a great man. If his ideas appear to-day somewhat reactionary, it must be remembered that he grew to manhood during the dark days of the French Revolution and the Napoleonic Wars, and that his period of influence in the government of Upper Canada coincided with that period of reaction in Europe when liberal ideas were everywhere at a discount. He made mistakes, but they were honest mistakes. He had opinions, but they were his

own opinions, sincerely held.   "For my
opinions," he once said, in his blunt way, "I
am responsible to no one."   That Upper
Canada, during its formative years, should
have come under the influence of such a man,
cannot be regarded as an unmixed evil; and
if he was a dominating figure in what is
called the "Family Compact," then the
"Family Compact" cannot have been as bad
as it has sometimes been painted.

There have recently been published some
of the letters of an English lady, the widow
of a Colonel Sibbald in the British army,
who came to Canada in 1837, and became a
friend of Bishop Strachan.   In a letter dated
April 20, 1861, Mrs. Sibbald writes:

"I called on the Bishop to congratulate him
on his 83rd birthday . . .   When shown
into the Library, there sat the Bishop in an
armchair, with a tabby cat as big as a dog on
his knees, the beast's two fore-paws nearly
reaching the Bishop's chin, and the head
resting on the paws.   As I entered, I said,
'Do you know, my lord, what I am come
about?' 'No, but I am glad to see you.'
'Well, this is your 83rd birthday, and I am
come to congratulate you.'   'Oh! then I
must have a kiss.'   So up he jumped for the

purpose, tumbling poor pussy on the ground."

Two and a half years later she writes:

"I perceive a great change in the dear old man since this time last year. He stoops more, and at my last visit he did not seem in his usual good spirits, complained that he was getting both deaf and blind, that his memory was failing him. I tried to console him by saying I also was getting deaf. 'I don't think that,' he said, 'for you can hear me, I perceive.' 'Oh, yes, my lord, and you hear me.' Then we agreed that it was not every one that spoke as plain, and then he chuckled and laughed."

Another year and a half elapsed, and we have a final glimpse of the aged Bishop, at the age of eighty-seven:

"The dear old Bishop, remembering I always paid him a visit on his birthday, sent Mrs. James Strachan in the morning of the last, asking me not to come, as the wind was extremely high, but that he would soon come to see me. He came the next day. He was not in his usual good spirits, as a Col. Gordon had just died, one of his oldest acquaintances. Hardly one now left of his own standing, as Judge McLean has been for some time on the brink of the grave, and is quite paralyzed. He asked me if I did not feel the difference in the change of society in Toronto since I first knew it?"

A year later Mrs. Sibbald died, at the age of eighty-three; and the Bishop, when he heard of her death, said, "With two old friends of our age it does not matter in the least who goes first; the other must soon follow." He had, throughout life, the habit of whistling to himself; and it is reported that he whistled to himself on this occasion.

Thus John Strachan faced the termination of his earthly course. His last days were typical of his whole life. He was a die-hard, who never knew when he was defeated. Many of the things for which he fought seem to us now wrong or unnecessary. In particular, his idea of the relation between Church and State is one which finds at present few exponents. He was stiff-necked and unconciliatory; and he was too contemptuous of opposition. But he had the root of the matter in him. He believed in religion and in education; and in the early days of Upper Canada his was a powerful influence working toward the recognition of the things of the spirit and the mind.

LORD SELKIRK

by

W. Martin

LORD SELKIRK

THOSE who have read *Ivanhoe* and *Kenilworth* are possibly not aware that the author had at least two ties binding him to Canada. A brother of Sir Walter Scott lived for some years at Niagara, the first capital of Upper Canada, and some who knew him said that he provided many of the plots for the novels which his brother Walter later wrote. Sir Walter Scott also knew the Earl of Selkirk in his boyhood, and in his diary frequently refers to him as one who "doffed the world aside and bid it pass!" Selkirk even asked Scott to join his venture, but the novelist was then forging fast ahead, and declined to forsake his pen. He was, however, greatly interested in Selkirk's spacious dreams.

Thomas Douglas, Lord Selkirk, was born in June, 1771, at the family seat, Kirkcudbrightshire, Scotland. He was the fifth son of the Earl of Selkirk. It is said that when Thomas was seven years old, his home was invaded by Captain Paul Jones, of the

New England States. The Captain had crossed the ocean in his ship, the *Ranger*, and harried the west coast of Great Britain. He worked north to the Scottish coast, which he knew well, as he had been born and bred in Kirkcudbrightshire. Coming to the home of the Selkirks, it was his intention to capture the head of the family. But by good fortune the Earl was away from home. This was during the American Revolution of 1776. Douglas was brought up amongst historic surroundings, and received a good education. He met at his home many of the outstanding men at that time; men like Sir Walter Scott and Robert Burns. At the age of fifteen he went to the University of Edinburgh, where he spent the next four years. While there he interested himself in the work of the various literary societies, and became a member of "The Club." It was here, too, that he formed a very intimate friendship with Sir Walter Scott, the great novelist.

THE FIGHT AT SEVEN OAKS

AS IF BITTER COLD, HUNGER, SICKNESS AND LONELINESS WERE NOT ENOUGH, THE SELKIRK SETTLERS FOUND THEMSELVES IN THE THICK OF THE OLD ENMITY BETWEEN THE HUDSON'S BAY COMPANY AND THE NOR'-WESTERS. LOOKING BACK, THE FIGHT AT SEVEN OAKS APPEARS SMALL ENOUGH, BUT IT WAS IMPORTANT IN RESULTS, AND DESERVES TO BE REMEMBERED AS ONE OF THE HISTORIC PLACES OF THE WEST.

Thomas Douglas showed himself to be a young man of energy and resourcefulness. After leaving the university he toured Europe, visiting especially France and Italy. While in Italy he studied the agriculture of that country, and wrote a pamphlet on it. France at this time was in the throes of the Revolution, and it was during this period, in company with many other young Britishers, that Douglas received the impressions that were no doubt a great factor in determining his later efforts at empire-building. His father died in 1799, and Thomas Douglas succeeded to the title as Earl of Selkirk, his four brothers having died before their father. There was much distress in Scotland at the time, the raising of sheep having driven many men from the farm, leaving them unemployed. Land was scarce, and people were starving, but here in Canada, lands were idle because of the lack of people to work them.

Lord Selkirk, having a good education,

possessing wealth and influence, turned his
thoughts towards relieving the distress in his
beloved country. He dreamed of noble projects. He laid plans for a systematic
scheme of emigration, having studied the
subject very carefully, and mastered the details. In his reading he came upon the romantic adventures of Alexander Mackenzie
and was fascinated by them. The long
treks through the wilderness made a great
impression on him. We have all been thrilled with the love of adventure, of going out
into the unknown, of looking around the
corner to see what new thing would present
itself, so that we can imagine how Selkirk
was challenged by the reading of Mackenzie's
exploits. Selkirk was a young man eighteen
years of age when Mackenzie started out on
his travels.

In this way Selkirk became interested in
Canada, and particularly in the Red River
valley, which he believed offered the advantage of good, fertile soil, and the opportu-

nity of securing it free of charge. The scheme which he prepared for the emigration of his Highlanders, was not only a plan for the relief of distress amongst them, but also for the broadening of the empire. Of this he said: "Now it is our duty to befriend this people. Let them be led abroad to new possessions. Let us direct their emigration; give them homes under our own flag, and they will strengthen the empire. No tract of land remains unoccupied on the sea-coast of the British America, except barren and frozen deserts. To find sufficient extent of good soil in a temperate climate, we must go far inland. This inconvenience, however, is not an insurmountable obstacle to the prosperity of a colony, and appears to be amply compensated for by other advantages that are to be found in some remote parts of British territory. At the western extremity of Canada, upon the waters which fall into Lake Winnipeg, and uniting with the great river of Port Nelson, discharge

LORD SELKIRK NAMING THE PARISH OF KILDONAN

"THE PARISH SHALL BE KILDONAN; HERE YOU SHALL BUILD YOUR CHURCH, AND THAT LOT IS FOR A SCHOOL."

themselves into Hudson Bay, is a fertile country, which the Indian traders represent as such, and of climate far more temperate than the shores of the Atlantic, under the same parallel, and not more severe than Germany or Poland. Here, therefore, the colonists may, with a moderate exertion of industry, be certain of a comfortable subsistence, and they may also raise some valuable objects of exportation."

This is a remarkable statement for that time (1802), because the average person looked upon the Canadian North West as "Polar Regions." Lord Selkirk made another striking prophecy. "It is a very moderate calculation to say that if these regions were occupied by an industrious population, they might afford ample means of subsistence for thirty millions of British subjects." How true this has become! Manitoba is now producing millions of bushels of wheat yearly, besides other products; while Winnipeg is one of the greatest wheat markets in the world, and the three prairie provinces are the granary of the empire.

Everyone seemed to oppose Lord Selkirk's emigration scheme, and the government actually forbade him to form a colony in what is now Manitoba. The prejudices of the British people were strongly against emigration, as Britain was engaged in a great war, and this project, they declared, would weaken her supply of men. Then, too, the Highland Society strenuously opposed the removal of Highlanders from their lands to the New World.

Selkirk's first attempt to establish a Scottish settlement was in Prince Edward Island. Eight hundred persons settled there, and experienced the usual difficulties and hardships of colonists. Many, however, became very prosperous farmers, and to-day thousands on the Island trace their descent from these Selkirk settlers. Lord Selkirk visited Prince Edward Island himself, and travelled through Eastern Canada and the United States. He then brought more settlers to Eastern Canada, but unfortunately these colonists were not so successful. In 1803 he visited Montreal, and was shown great hospitality by the "Beaver Club." This was an organization which limited its membership to those who dealt in furs. Every meeting meant a banquet, and each club-man wore a gold medal on which was engraved the motto, *Fortitude in Distress*. Dishes were served which smacked of the prairie and forest. After the toasts had been drunk, the jovial party knelt on the floor for a final ceremony. With poker or tongs, or whatever else was at hand, they imitated paddlers in action, and a chorus of lusty voices joined in a burst of song! One can imagine Selkirk asking eager questions of the "Beavers," for nothing escaped his keen observation.

When thirty-six years of age Selkirk married a Miss Jane Colville, whose family were influential people, and connected with the Hudson's Bay Company. Lady Selkirk was a very practical woman, and helped her husband a great deal with his emigration schemes. Her sympathy and co-operation were invaluable. The North West Company, a rival fur-trading organization, bitterly opposed Selkirk's land settlement idea. They believed that he would not be able to carry his plan through, for to them it appeared to be the mad act of an impractical dreamer. In 1808, Selkirk, having proved the validity of the Hudson's Bay charter, bought a large amount of stock in the Company, and became a Director. He tried to persuade the Company to colonize with him, but they refused. Selkirk then proposed that if they would give the land, he would people this within a given period, at his own expense, foster the early efforts of the settlers, and appease the claims of the Indian tribes that inhabited the territory.

In 1811, the Hudson's Bay Company

gave him 116,000 square miles of land, covering what is now Manitoba and part of the states of Minnesota and North Dakota. You will understand that at this date the boundary line in the North West was not yet fixed between Canada and the United States. Selkirk's friends and acquaintances did not know what to think of this scheme. Some thought it absurd. One man meeting him in London said: "If you are bent on doing something futile, why don't you sow tares at home, in order to reap wheat; or plough up the desert of Sahara, which is nearer?" However, Selkirk was determined, and immediately advertised for settlers. Here is the gist of his prospectus.

"Land was to be given away free, or sold for a nominal sum. To the poor, transportation would cost nothing; others would have to pay according to their means. No one would be debarred on account of their religion, and all creeds were to be treated alike."

Selkirk met with a good deal of opposition, for in the meantime the North West Company agents had been very busy, trying to dissuade the people from going. A pamphlet was written and published which was designed to care off prospective settlers by warning of the perils that faced those wishing to settle there. An unhappy picture was painted of a land hostile in the extreme: neither the people living there nor the climate would provide a welcome.

The Selkirk party of about ninety people was finally gathered together, however, and late in July, 1811, the Hudson's Bay Company ships, *Prince of Wales* and *Eddystone,* with the transport *Edward and Ann*, were ready for the trip. The voyage took sixty-one days, a very lengthy period, even for those days. The ships were in poor condition, badly manned and ill-equipped, and much stormy weather was encountered. On September 24th they landed at York Factory, near Fort Nelson. Winter was fast approaching, and it was too late to proceed to their final destination. One can imagine what their thoughts must have been! Strangers in a strange land, without home or shelter, yet they came of a race that nothing daunts. This brave little party, men, women and children, (numbering in all, one hundred and five) landed on the inhospitable shores of Hudson Bay, unpopulated by civilized creatures, with the exception of the Fur Traders at their scattered posts, Indians and Métis. They were, however, undaunted by the prospect before them. They knew that they had to travel several hundred miles before they could reach their "Land of Promise," a journey full of peril, not only from wild beasts, but from hostile Indians fearing threats to their way of life.

Then, too, they had to look forward to the intense cold of the northern winter, and prepare themselves for its severity as quickly as possible. Haste was imperative! There was no accommodation for them at York

Factory, and log houses had to be built. Macdonnell, Selkirk's agent, took charge of this work, and superintended the building of winter quarters. These were completed by October 26th. The men were awkward with the axe, and equally unskilled with the rifle. They were all kept busy enough during the winter, hunting deer and partridges for food, and cutting firewood. The time passed without serious mishap. Towards spring they had to build large, flat boats, or *bateaux*, to convey themselves, their families, and their belongings, by river and lake, to their final destination.

The party left York Factory early in July, 1812. Up Hayes River, up the whole length of Lake Winnipeg they travelled, and then in August, after many portages and treacherous rapids, the boats ascended the muddy current of the Red River, flowing through what is now known as Manitoba. For the first time, the people saw their promised land! Through the trees fringing the river broken glimpses could be had of the prairie, a vast, gently billowing sea of green, washed in sunlight and fragrant air, stretching as far as the eye could see to where the sky stoops down to meet the earth.

At last their *bateaux* were drawn up St. Andrew's Rapids, where the locks are now situated, while Indians, from the vicinity of the Fort, regarded with wonder these white-faced new-comers, who had crossed the "great waters to dig gardens and work lands."

The Selkirk settlers arrived at Fort Douglas, so called after the family name of the earl, and the site of the present city of Winnipeg, on August 30th, 1812. Scarcely had they taken stock of their new surroundings, when they were chilled to the marrow with terror. Towards them, riding swiftly on horseback, came a formidable looking troop, decked in all the war accoutrements of the Indian, spreading feathers, dangling tomahawk, each wearing a thick, terrifying coat of war paint. To the new-comers it was a never-to-be-forgotten spectacle! But when the riders came within close range, shouting and gesticulating as they came, it was seen that they wore borrowed apparel, and that they were a band of Métis people of mixed Indian and French blood, disguised to appear as fierce and forbidding as possible. Their object was to tell Lord Selkirk's party that settlers were not wanted on the Red River, that it was the country of the fur trader, and that settlers must go farther afield.

Governor Miles Macdonell, of the Hudson's Bay Company, planned a ceremony for the official inauguration of Lord Selkirk's Colony. At the appointed hour on September 24th, several traders from Fort Gibraltar, the North West post, together with a few French-Canadians and Indians, put in an appearance. In the presence of this odd company, Macdonell read Lord Selkirk's patent to Assiniboia. About him

were drawn a guard of honour, and overhead
the British Ensign floated in the breeze.
Six small swivel guns, which had been
brought with the colonists, belched forth a
salute to mark the occasion. The Nor'-
Westers were visibly impressed by this show
of authority and power.

Much might be written of the colonists'
first year in this new country. We know
something of the joys and sorrows of these
early years, of the sufferings and the splendid fortitude of these early settlers; how the
rude Plain Rangers conveyed them to the
buffalo hunt in their wildly creaking Red
River carts; or how, on loaded ponies, many
a young Highlander came to grief in the
wild stampede of his first buffalo hunt!
Many a happy winter night was passed in
dancing wild Indian jigs, to the stirring
skirl of the Highland pipes, or the sawing
and scraping of some French fiddler.

When spring opened, ten-acre lots were
assigned to each settler, close to the Fort, at

what were known as the Colony Gardens, and one hundred-acre farms farther down the river. The North West Company were envious of, and feared this hardy, enterprising Scottish settlement, and did their best to destroy the colony. They almost succeeded. The instructions given to their chief were, that "Selkirk must be driven to abandon his project at any cost, for his colony would prove destructive to our fur trade."

Selkirk replied in kind. He wrote the Governor of his colony that, "The North West Company must be compelled to quit my lands. If they refuse they must be treated as poachers." Selkirk believed that the vast territory granted to him was legally his own property, as much as his parks in Scotland. He believed that he possessed the same right to expel intruders on this territory, as to drive poachers form his own Scotch estates. This was the spirit of Feudalism. The Nor'-Westers, on the other hand, claimed that the charter of the Hudson's Bay Company did not apply beyond the bounds of Hudson Bay. Even if it did hold good beyond those limits, they pointed out that, by the terms of the charter, it applied only to lands not possessed by any other Christian power. And who would dispute that French fur traders and their successors, the Nor'-Westers, had ascended the streams of the interior long before the Hudson's Bay Company men? This was the spirit of Democracy. It needed no prophet to foresee that, when these claims met, there would be a violent clash.

At this point it would be well to note the difference between the leading rival companies, the Hudson's Bay factors, and those of the North West Company, in their method of trading with the Indians. It was the custom of the Hudson's Bay men to trade with the Indians through a window, and to discourage all friendly relations between them and the white men at the Post. The

Governor even beat one man with his cane for going into an Indian tent to light his pipe! On the other hand, the traders of the North West Company went freely amongst the Indians, making lavish use of rum and spirits. The result of this difference in treatment was that the latter took out many more furs than their rivals.

The thrilling story of each year, with its plot and counterplot, would fill a large volume. In spite of Nor'-Westers' threats, in spite of the fact that there would be no market for the colonists when they had succeeded in transforming the prairie wilderness into farms, Selkirk's "mad" dream of Empire seemed about to be realized. It had long been his wish to visit this colony, and in 1815 he arrived in Montreal with Lady Selkirk. The winter of 1815-16 had been a disastrous one for the settlers. The North West Company had nearly succeeded in wiping out the little colony. McLeod, of the Hudson's Bay Company, states (in his journal) that all the colonists' houses were destroyed by fire. Homeless, wounded, and in extreme distress they took to the boats, and saving what they could, started for Norway House, declaring they would never return.

Robert Semple brought out a new party to the colony to succeed these, but in June, 1816, Governor Semple and a party of twenty-one men were killed by some Métis at Seven Oaks, a spot marked by a stone monument just three miles north of the present City Hall, Winnipeg.

The Senior Officer of the North West Company now took up his residence in the late Governor Semple's apartments, and tried by every means to win over the Indians from their loyalty to the settlers. He addressed the Salteaux tribe, but Pequis, their chief, listened in stony silence, refusing to be moved from his allegiance, for he had been a friend of Governor Semple's. To mark his lasting friendship for the Selkirk settlers, a statue has recently been erected to Chief Pequis in Kildonan Park, Winnipeg.

Lord Selkirk arrived at Fort William soon after the incident and immediately took drastic measures. Acting as a Justice of the Peace, he held a court in which the Nor'-Westers, represented by William McGillivray, their western chief, were tried for their alleged crimes against the Selkirk settlers, which had culminated in the tragedy at Seven Oaks. Before the day was over, Selkirk had sufficient evidence, as he thought, to justify legal actions against certain parties, partners of the North West Company at Fort William. McGillivray was first arrested, and then the remaining partners at Fort William. These men were sent east for trial. Selkirk now proceeded on his way to the western settlement. He left Fort William on May 1st, and after an uneventful journey by canoe, he reached Fort Douglas at the end of June.

His thoughts must indeed have been sad on first nearing the ground for which so much blood had been shed, and for which he himself was to suffer so much. One may venture to say that in his most daring dreams, Selkirk never imagined the extent to which this part of the Empire was to grow from the seed he had planted. At Fort Douglas he was met by the colonists in council, and greeted by them as their friend and protector. During the following weeks he put the colony on a proper organized footing, even to the extent of planning for an experimental farm. While in the West Lord Selkirk fully gained the respect and loyalty of the Indians, and as a token of their admiration they bestowed upon him the title of "The Silver Chief."

Selkirk was anxious to acquire the ancient title which the Indians held to the lands of Assiniboia, in order to prevent future disputes. To effect this he brought together

at Fort Douglas a body of chiefs who represented the Cree and Salteaux nations. The
Indian chiefs made eloquent speeches. They
said that they were willing to surrender their
claim to a strip of land, two miles in width,
on either side of the Red River, from the
mouth to the Red Lake River (now Grand
Forks, North Dakota), and on either side
of the Assiniboine as far as its junction with
the Muskrat. This was measured by seeing
how much land could be seen under a horse's
belly towards the horizon. At Fort Douglas,
Fort Daer, and at the junction of the Red
and Red Lake Rivers, Selkirk secured about
six miles on either side of the river. A peaceful treaty was concluded and the usual
presents distributed. In signing the treaty,
several chiefs drew odd pictures of animals
on a rough map of the territory in question.
These animals were their respective totems,
and were placed opposite the region over
which they claimed territory. It was stipu-

lated that one hundred pounds of good to-
bacco should be given annually to each
nation as a special gift.

One sunny day in August, 1817, Selkirk
gathered his settlers about him and said:
"The parish shall be Kildonan; here you
shall build your church, and that lot (indi-
cating a piece of ground) is for a school."
In September he left the colony, and travelled
south by way of the United States. Upon
arriving in the East he found himself pursued by officers of the law, and immediately
legal proceedings began. These were carried on for a long time by both parties. The
trials were both tiresome and very dis-
heartening to Selkirk. Money was spent
without stint, and much influence brought
to bear by the North West Company to fight
Selkirk's charges. These charges, which
included burglary, arson, robbery and mur-
der, were not proven, and Selkirk had to pay
large amounts of money in fines and costs.
Failing health now compelled him to leave

Canada, with his wife and family, for England. Recovered in health he contemplated further legal action against the North West Company, but again he became very ill. He went to Pau, in the south of France, where he lived but a short time, and died in 1820, being buried under the shadows of the Pyrenees.

It is an interesting coincidence that Sir Alexander Mackenzie and Lord Selkirk, to both of whom we owe so much for opening up the great western country, died the same year, the former on March 12th, and the latter on April 8th.

The Hudson's Bay Company shortly afterwards bought back the rights that lay in Canada, and that Company and the North West Company were united in 1821. This union of the rival Companies was a prophecy of that peace on the plains, out of which was to develop a great western tradition of strength and peace.

Lord Selkirk's name will always remain

inseparably connected with the western country. He was generous with his wealth, and lavish with his love for mankind. His emigration enterprise cost him over half a million dollars. All his schemes were philanthropic. He aimed to help others by assisting them to help themselves, to improve living conditions, and to leave this world a better place. To show how Selkirk had lavished his money on this scheme, we find, after his death, the Selkirk estates were encumbered with a debt of £160,000, and that his account with his financial agents in Montreal was overdrawn to the extent of more than £10,000.

Half a century after Selkirk's death the British Government began to see the promise in the West! Half a century later the Canadian provinces were convinced of the necessity of extending the boundaries of the Dominion to the Pacific.

Consider, for a moment, the settlement that Selkirk established. It may be claimed that he followed in the path of the great explorers, but that he made no fresh discoveries. He undertook to colonize territory already in the possession of others, all of it well known. His settlement dwindled almost to the vanishing point, and never at any time was an important factor in trade. Some even assert that he was, in spite of his kindness and generosity, unreasonable and, on occasion, unscrupulous. However that may be, his name has become a tradition in Canada. Those pioneer struggles have left something priceless in the blood of the race, that makes for national greatness and character. Heroism leaves nothing insignificant that it touches! And so it happens that these humble immigrants, although a century has rolled between them and us, to-day take their place among the imperishable names on our nation's Roll of Honour!

Recall, again, their means of communication, and compare them with ours. Time has wrought miracles! The express canoes of the brigade of York boats once furnished a most picturesque spectacle. The voyageurs, with their brightly coloured shirts, proud feathers, and gay, streaming ribbons, then dipped their glittering paddles in the Red River, to the tune of old French river-songs. These have passed; and in their place the swift river steamer ploughs the waters. Transcontinental trains roar along, waking echoes among the historic old trails. Overhead, against the sun, hums an aeroplane, disputing the kingdom of the eagle. Telegraph and telephone usurp the packet of the *coureur,* while the air throbs with melody and is electric with news, flashed from radios below the horizon!

Let us look once again at the little hamlet, a mere trading post, in a vast plain midway between the Atlantic and the Pacific, struggling feebly for its existence. Then think of Winnipeg, proud city of the plains, rearing its great buildings on the spot where, for long years, the Red River colony battled natives, loneliness, and obstacles enough to break the hearts of all but heroes. All honour to the dauntless men and brave women of the Selkirk settlement!

Thomas Douglas, Earl of Selkirk, so splendidly endowed with lofty dreams, and brotherly love, was the inspiration of those early pioneers, who well and truly laid the foundation of a new country. The body of Lord Selkirk sleeps with his forbears, but his brave spirit walks the ramparts of his dreams in The Empire on the Plains!

SAMUEL CUNARD

by

Archibald MacMechan

SAMUEL CUNARD

THE CUNARD family is of German origin. In 1683, Thones Kunders emigrated from Crefeld to Philadelphia, where he was granted land by William Penn himself. His great-grandson, Abraham Cunard, came to Halifax some time before 1785. He was a carpenter by trade, and obtained employment in the Dock Yard. His wife's maiden name was Margaret Murphy. She came with a band of Loyalists from South Carolina, to whom a large tract of land, in Nova Scotia, was granted in 1784. This township was called Rawdon, in honour of Lord Rawdon, the victor over Gates at Camden, and afterwards Governor-General of India. The settlers of Rawdon seem to have been soldiers who fought under the celebrated general. In a small house which, until recently, stood behind 257 Brunswick Street, the Cunards' second child was born, November 21st, 1787, and named Samuel, for his paternal grandfather. The property running down the steep hill to the harbour was, for many years, in the possession of the Cunard family; at the foot they built the wharf and warehouse long known by their name.

His father's education was scanty, but Samuel went to school, and proved an apt scholar. He probably attended the Halifax Grammar School, of which Parson George Wright was headmaster. Wright was missionary to the Germans, and rector of Saint George's Church in Brunswick Street, about a stone's throw from the Cunard house. In this church Samuel Cunard's family pew is still pointed out. Local tradition tells how little Sam drove the family cow to and from the pasture, knitting a sock as he walked along, and how he would take his basket after school and gather dandelions. These he would sell for what he could get. With his gains he would attend the nightly auctions, and bid in bargains, to be sold later at a profit.

After leaving school, he obtained a post in the Civil Branch of the Engineering Estab-

After an old engraving by Day and Haghe, Lithographers to the King, 17 Crate St., Lincoln's Inn Fields.

SAMUEL CUNARD STANDING AT DARTMOUTH POINT: TO THE LEFT LIES THE ENTRANCE TO HALIFAX HARBOUR; THE MILITARY HOSPITAL STANDS ON THE EASTERN SLOPES OF CITADEL HILL, WHICH IS CROWNED BY THE CITADEL ITSELF.

lishment. His father had risen to the rank of master carpenter in the Dock Yard, a position which involved contacts with navy and army officials. It seems probable that Samuel obtained his first job through his father's influence. The inference is that his education must have been good. A clerk who was not neat and accurate, business-like and good at figures would be valueless in the office of the scientific branch of the Army. There must have been plenty of work—drafting, copying, making plans—in the Engineers' Office in the Lumber Yard, for Britain was at war all through Samuel Cunard's boyhood and young manhood. He must have seen the town illuminated for Nelson's victories, and shared the patriotic thrills at the triumphs in the Peninsula. Halifax was an important naval base, heavily garrisoned, and the Forces were commanded for six years by a Prince of the Blood. Halifax prospered, especially during the closing years of the great struggle. Some time towards the end of the war, presumably between 1809 and 1813, the master-carpenter went into partnership with his clever, thrifty, well-educated eldest son, who had already established a reputation for reliability. The foundation of the Cunard fortunes is said to have been the purchase of a prize, not a large vessel, but a good bargain. The Halifax *Weekly Chronicle* of July 2, 1813, contains an advertisement of a new firm, A. Cunard and Son. They are agents for the ship *White Oak*, loading for London. The names of father and son also appear in the long list of subscribers to the Royal Acadian Society; they engage to pay a pound a piece, annually, to support Bromley's new school. Next year, the firm advertises the arrival of a cargo of rum and sugar from the West Indies. A very old Halifax lady remembered "Sam" Cunard as a young man carrying his money in a stocking instead of the long, netted purse of the period, and getting up in the morning, when the rest of Halifax was asleep, and buying to advantage schooner loads of fish and potatoes. Thrift and the trading instinct were ingrained in him.

Waterloo year was an important date in Cunard's life. On February 4th, 1815, he married Susan, daughter of William Duffus, and their first child was born on the last day of December. The firm of A. Cunard and Son is so prosperous that it is able to make the handsome donation of thirty pounds to the Waterloo Fund. From this time on, Samuel becomes more and more prominent in the affairs of his native city.

The long war which ended with Waterloo was followed by a long period of depression. The year 1816 was the year without a summer. In 1819 the Dock Yard establishment was removed to Bermuda, at the whim of an admiral. In 1820 soup-kitchens were needed in Halifax to tide the poor people through the hard winter. According to Chittick, this local depression lasted twenty years, and ended in a money panic; but throughout it all Cunard prospered. He becomes a leading citizen, he administers Lord Dalhousie's bounty to the destitute emigrants; he is appointed Commissioner of Lighthouses; he becomes captain in the fashionable Second Halifax Regiment of Militia, and eventually rises to command it; he is a Fire Ward of the North Suburbs, and a member of the exclusive Sun Fire Company. Cunard's wharf is the centre of the West India trade, and the firm keeps Lyle and Chappell, of Dartmouth, busy building ships for it, and giving employment to hundreds of men. John Cunard is master of one of their vessels.

A brief matter-of-fact paragraph in a corner of *The Weekly Chronicle,* of April 19, 1821, throws light on the Cunard method. It is headed simply "Dispatch," in small capitals, and runs thus: "The brig *Mary-Ann,* J. Cunard, master, entered at the Customs House on Monday, the 9th inst., discharged her cargo, 124 puns. rum and 4 hhds. sugar—took on board a full cargo of fish, staves, etc., and sailed again on

Wednesday last, April 11th, at 3 o'clock,
having completed the whole business of un-
loading, receiving and stowing a cargo in
two and one-quarter days. The brig is
owned by A. Cunard and Son, of this
town." At that time and long afterwards,
the regular working hours were from daylight till dark. Cunard exemplifies the ancient
Hebrew proverb: "Seest thou a man diligent
in his business? he shall stand before kings;
he shall not stand before mean men."

The year 1820 is another important date
in Cunard's career. He bought his parents
a huge farm at Rawdon, whither they
retired to end their days in peace and comfort. Soon after, the firm changed its name
to S. Cunard and Company, and engaged
in the whale fishery. In this year, also,
he opened a house in Chatham, N.B.,
for the lucrative timber trade, which did "an
enormous business" for twenty-eight years.
It was conducted by his brothers Joseph and
Henry.

This branch built ships, "eight or ten,

THE *BRITANNIA* ARRIVES AT HALIFAX ON HER MAIDEN VOYAGE

annually," caught, cured and exported fish; manufactured bricks. Joseph went into the Legislature and lived in his mansion at Chatham in great state. Samuel Cunard also bought large tracts of land in Prince Edward Island, and he was engaged in the iron works erected at Clementsport. His wide interests did not interfere with civic duties. Along with Michael Tobin, he administered poor relief during the hard winter of 1820-21, when Halifax Harbour was frozen over for weeks.

Within the next few years, he has advanced still further. In 1825 his name appears as one of the founders of the Halifax Banking Company. Projects for establishing a local bank had been mooted for years; at last the much needed aid to business came into being. In the same year S. Cunard and Company figure as agents for the Honourable East India Company. The first direct shipment of tea, 6,517 chests, in the *Countess of Harcourt*, reached Halifax on May 29th, 1825, in four months, from

Canton. The arrival of this cargo was hailed with delight. It meant cheaper tea for the multitude. It also made S. Cunard and Co. the distributors of tea for British North America. William J. Stairs, as a boy, remembered Mr. Cunard himself auctioning the lots in the huge, iron-stone warehouse built at the head of the wharf specially to contain these importations. He recalled the great man's "brisk step, his quick and ready movements," and his own pleasure at being noticed and identified by the local magnate. The teas were catalogued before the sale.

In 1826 Cunard offered himself for election to the Legislative Assembly; but he was not successful. Politics was not his forte. In this same year he showed his deep interest in the idea with which his name is for ever associated—steam navigation. A local company was formed to operate steam vessels between Halifax and Quebec. He made one of the committee to solicit subscriptions, and he himself subscribed a thousand pounds towards the enterprise. It is therefore evident that his great project, which made him world-famous, arose from no sudden impulse, but was long in maturing, and grew out of tested experience.

It is difficult to make a complete list of Cunard's interests and activities. For years a plan of linking up the waterways across the province had been under consideration. It was the age of canal building in England. The Shubenacadie Canal Company was formed and duly incorporated. Its charter is dated June 1st, 1826. Few local undertakings of the period were more ambitious. The canal would be more than fifty-three miles long, and would cost seventy-five thousand pounds. It would tap the resources of the interior; it would link Fundy with the Atlantic; it would prove useful in war. Cunard subscribed £1,000 towards the undertaking.

In January, 1828, his wife died; he never married again. He was remembered by the parishioners of St. George's, the "Round

Church," in his pew Sunday after Sunday, with his motherless children.

In 1830 he was appointed to the Legislative Council, the irresponsible second chamber, whose power Howe was destined to overthrow. This means his formal recognition as a leading citizen by the junta of officials and rich merchants who controlled the city and the province. At this time he was estimated as being worth not less than two hundred thousand pounds, and the firm had a fleet of forty sail under their control. Henceforth he is the Honourable Samuel Cunard; but he seems to have taken little interest in politics, even when the Reform agitation convulsed Nova Scotia, and it was noted that Howe never attacked him. His continued interest in steam navigation is evinced by his subscribing to the construction of the *Royal William*. The keel of this vessel was laid in 1830, and she was completed the next year. She was designed to ply between Quebec and Halifax. First in the list of the one hundred and forty-four subscribers stands the name of Samuel Cunard. In 1833 she made her famous voyage across the Atlantic, and, despite the rival claims of the *Savannah* and the *Sirius*, was the first to cross the ocean under steam propulsion.

In 1827 the General Mining Association, a powerful English organization, obtained control of large coal areas in Cape Breton; and some time later S. Cunard and Company became the local agents. This was an important and profitable arrangement, like the agency for the East India Company. As long as the Cunard steamers called at Halifax, inward and outward bound, they filled their bunkers with G.M.A. coal.

The business of Samuel Cunard had spread out in all directions, not only in his native province, but in the West Indies, Prince Edward Island and New Brunswick, with various relationships in Great Britain. The correspondence must have been enormous; indeed, it took three months to burn the firm's papers when the wharf was acquired by the Intercolonial Railway. Communication had to be made without the modern aids of steam, telegraph, cable, wireless. It was slow and most uncertain. Winds might be adverse to the slow sailing packets, or fail them altogether. Regular, punctual exchange of letters was impossible; but regularity and punctuality are of the very essence of business. According to family tradition, Cunard had discussed ocean transport of mail, by steam, with Richard Brown, the scientific expert of G.M.A., long before, in his office at Sydney. No doubt he discussed it with many persons, who fretted at the same inconveniences. The image in Cunard's mind was the regularity of a railway; and he applied the figure to ocean transportation. His two little schooners, the *Lady Ogle* and the *Lady Strange*, were conveying the mails between Halifax, Newfoundland, Boston and Bermuda. With that achievement went the plying of coastal steamers in which he was interested. His opportunity came in 1839, when he was fifty-two years of age.

The previous year, 1838, is notable in the history of ocean travel. In that year two vessels crossed the Atlantic and returned, under steam propulsion. One was the *Sirius*, an English steamer plying in coastal waters. Her trip was made as an experiment, in satisfaction of a challenge. On her return trip she overhauled and passed the packet *Tyrian*, conveying the mails from Halifax to Falmouth. The *Tyrian* was lying becalmed, a log upon the sea, with canvas idly flapping, and waiting for a breeze. Captain Jennings signalled the new-fangled steam vessel to stop, and he transferred the mail-bags, "pormanteaus," to the hold of the *Sirius*. Soon the odd-looking little paddle-wheel steamer, with the dog and star for figurehead, was again under way. Again the paddle-wheels churned the windless sea, and soon her tall, smoking "chimney," reaching almost to the cross-trees of her two masts, had vanished beyond the sky-line.

This object lesson on the speedy conveyance of mails was not lost on two of the *Tyrian's* passengers, Joseph Howe, on his first trip to Europe, and Thomas Chandler Haliburton, going to be lionized in London as the creator of "Sam Slick." On reaching London, these two staunch friends of Nova Scotia made common cause with Henry Bliss and William Crane, of New Brunswick, in urging upon the British Government the importance of rapid communication between the old world and the new, by means of steam. Howe addressed an able letter to Lord Glenelg on the subject, which seems to have given a final prod to the government. That autumn they advertised for tenders for the regular conveyance of mails by steam vessels across the Atlantic. There was only one tender, that of the successful colonial merchant, Samuel Cunard.

At once, he "interested" the most prominent steamship owners, and formed a new company, "The British and North American Royal Mail Steam Packet Company," with a capital of £270,000, to which S. Cunard and Company subscribed about one-fifth. The contract called for three steam vessels, of specified size, power and quality, to be delivered at fixed dates. There were to be two sailings each month. The contract was for seven years; it was signed on March 18th, 1839, and next year the first Cunarder made her first voyage.

Certain modifications were made in the original plans of the government. Instead of starting from Falmouth, near Land's End, thereby avoiding the difficult navigation up Channel, the new vessels were to start from the rising shipping centre, Liverpool. Instead of small vessels for mails only, they were to be large enough to carry passengers with suitable accommodations. These changes were due to Cunard himself, at the suggestion of Mr. Napier, of Glasgow.

In the meantime, terminals had to be built at Boston. In the 1830's, Boston was a small town. Noddle's Island, now East Boston, was just beginning to be reclaimed. In 1835 there were only six hundred inhabitants in the whole district. The company built a new wharf and warehouse there at a cost of £10,000. The coming of this pioneer line of steamers to Boston was an event of prime importance to the city, and its withdrawal in 1868 was felt to be a severe blow.

The first of the line was the *Britannia*. She was a wooden, paddle-wheel steamer with three masts, carrying fore-and-aft sails on all three, and crossing two square yards on both the fore and the main masts. Her length was only a little over two hundred feet, and she measured eleven hundred and fifty-four tons. She could steam at 8.5 knots an hour, with an engine of 740 horse-power. Dickens, who came out in her in January, 1842, has immortalized "the far-famed American steamer" in the first two chapters of *American Notes*. A wooden vessel could not be large; the weakness of the material of which it was built, and the rough usage of the sea, limited its dimensions. The early marine engines were weak. It was the breakdown of her engines which caused the tragedy of the *London* in a Biscay gale. The paddle-wheel in its paddle-box was easily disabled by a heavy sea; the "floats" could be torn off. After some bad weather Dickens came on deck to find that "The planking of the paddle-boxes had been torn sheer away. The wheels were exposed and bare; and they whirled and dashed their spray about the decks at random. . . . The lifeboat had been crushed by one blow of the sea like a walnut shell, and there it hung dangling in the air: a mere faggot of crazy boards."

The *Britannia* sailed from Liverpool on July 4th, 1840. Cunard himself was on board, and the passenger list included some sixty persons. She reached Halifax early on the morning of the 17th, made a very short stay at this port, and proceeded to

Boston, which she reached on the 21st of the month.

The Bostonians celebrated the event with enthusiasm. In front of the new Maverick House a huge pavilion was erected, in which a dinner was given for two thousand persons. Cunard was the guest of honour. The Governor of the State presided; the pavilion was decorated with flags, emblems, and the names of the three ports now joined by steam. Long was the list of toasts, speeches and songs. Cunard's health was drunk; but his response was a formal expression of thanks. He never was a speaker. But the gathering included Daniel Webster, the famous orator, and he was called on for a speech. The frank reporter more than suggests that it was commonplace. It ended in a somewhat truculent toast.

But this was not all. The enthusiastic Bostonians subscribed five thousand dollars for a silver vase, and presented it to Samuel Cunard. It is decorated with dolphins, shells, anchors and other marine emblems, and bears on the side a faithful image of the *Britannia* cleaving the waves. It is their tribute to his "enterprise" in establishing the line of British mail steam packets between Liverpool, Halifax and Boston.

So the line was founded, and it flourished for the seven years of the first contract. The British Government paid a subsidy of £150,000 a year. Carrying passengers was profitable. Carrying cargoes of fine, valuable goods was even more profitable. In 1845 the duty paid on the cargoes of the *Cambria* and the *Hibernia* was $100,000 each. The benefit to business in the speedy and regular delivery of mails across the Atlantic was quite incalculable, not only to the mercantile interests of Boston, but to Canada. The old Halifax-Quebec route was given up, and mails were sent by rail to Montreal. This led the way to granting the bonding privilege by which goods of all kinds may be shipped through the United

States to Canada without examination for duty; and this privilege was obtained through Cunard's personal exertions at Washington. In 1846 there was some difficulty in renewing the contract with the government; but Cunard secured it because no other firm would undertake to run steamships, on time, in the winter. In the same year he was made a Fellow of the Royal Geographical Society.

Samuel Cunard's successful career was not without its shadows. In 1848 the branch of the firm at Chatham, N.B., failed. The failure was due to a loose, extravagant way of doing business, according to local critics. Joseph Cunard provided dramatic scenes, spurring his horse through the excited crowd, with pistols in his boots. The firm assigned to Robert McCalmont, Samuel Cunard and Thomas C. Allen, Manager of the Commercial Bank at Newcastle. By 1871 the last claims of the creditors were fully met. For a time S. Cunard and Company were in difficulties, from which they ultimately recovered. Cunard died a rich man.

The year 1848 also dates Cunard's removal to London, where he spent the remainder of his life. In 1854 the Crimean War broke out. After the long peace, the War Department was unprepared for such an emergency, and much confusion resulted in transporting the forces, supplies, etc., to the seat of war. Indeed, the Crimean War is almost a synonym for official muddle and mismanagement. Samuel Cunard put all the available steamers of the line at the disposal of the Government, with "no haggle of price, no driving a good bargain for the Company," writes an admiring friend. The same authority adds, "The Cunard fleet made good work up the Mediterranean, landing men and stores more promptly and with better delivery than the Government transports had done. This brought good pay for the Company." Official recognition of Cunard's generous and patriotic service took the form of a baronetcy conferred on him throughout Palmerston in 1859. He was now Sir Samuel Cunard. This title was the crown of his life work; the poor carpenter's son had been admitted to the ranks of the British aristocracy. He died in his London residence, April 28th, 1865, in his seventy-eighth year. Lincoln had been assassinated a fortnight previously; the papers were ringing with the tragedy, and little notice was taken of the quiet demise of Sir Samuel Cunard, Bart.

In person, Samuel Cunard was a little man, well made, alert, and brisk in his movements. The portrait by which he is best known is of a handsome man, with vigor, decision and ability written on his firm features. A Halifax merchant wrote of him: "He was a skilful diplomatist—I have thought, looking at little Lord John Russell, whom he personally resembled (though of a larger mould) that he was the ablest man of the two. . . . He was a very able man, and, I am happy to say, I believe

also a good man. In early life he was somewhat imperious. He believed in himself—
he made both men and things bend to his
will." But he mellowed with age. Cunard
was not a talker; he was a doer, a man of
action; but some of his significant utterances
have been preserved.

He held that "steamers properly built and
manned might start and arrive at their destination with the punctuality of railway
trains on land." Indeed, his favourite figure
was "ocean railway"; the underlying idea
being regularity of service, in contrast to the
maddening irregularity inseparable from the
days of sail. To Samuel Cunard belongs
all the honour of the daring pioneer who
pushes out into unknown regions. It was
as if some one had contracted for an air-mail
service between London and Paris, immediately after Blériot's flight across the Channel. He was the pioneer of transatlantic
steam transportation and travel. He had
high hopes for the future of his native city.
He predicted that "the day would surely

come when an ocean steamer would be signalled from Citadel Hill every day of the year."

He left a lasting impression on the famous line which bears his name. It has an unrivalled reputation for safety. Up to the Great War, it could truly boast that it "never lost a passenger." The phrase became almost a proverb on shipboard, almost a joke; and it would seem that this reputation is traceable to the founder of the line. From the first, it was his steadfast resolve to have "nothing but the best ships, the best officers and the best men." Rules embodying this principle were formed, and have been followed, to the great benefit of those who travel by sea. Their origin was in the character of "the small, grey-haired man of quiet manners and not overflowing speech," the poor boy who made the most of his opportunities in Halifax a century ago.

SIR SANDFORD FLEMING

by

Lawrence J. Burpee

SIR SANDFORD FLEMING

SANDFORD FLEMING was born in Kirkcaldy, Scotland, on January 7th, 1827. He was educated at the Kirkcaldy Burgh School, of which Carlyle had been master some twenty years or so before. Here in the Lang Toun, straggling, picturesque in its way, filled with a shrewd, hard-headed, and hard-working population, Sandford Fleming spent his boyhood days. It nurtured in him that rare combination of gifts, the genius for dreaming great dreams and the capacity for making them realities. Here were planted in his mind the germs of mighty projects, destined to be developed in the course of time under other and distant skies.

Fleming developed early those qualities of thoroughness and stickativeness that were to become marked features of his character. He began about this time to keep a diary. Most boys do that, but in the vast majority of cases the diary enjoys but a very short life. Fleming's diary was carried on year after year throughout his long life.

In the very first of these diaries one finds

written in a boyish hand this extract from *Poor Richard's Almanack:* "But dost thou love life? Then do not squander time for that is the stuff life is made of. How much more than is necessary do we spend in sleep, forgetting that the sleeping fox catches no poultry, and that there will be sleeping enough in the grave. Sloth maketh all things difficult but industry all easy; and he that riseth late must trot all day and shall scarcely overtake his business at night; while laziness travels so slow that poverty soon overtakes him." Not to squander time was one of the guiding principles of Sandford Fleming's life. It made that life a full one in the broadest and best sense of the term.

On his eighteenth birthday an entry in the diary makes it clear that the young man's thoughts were turning toward Canada. By dint of hard work he had qualified himself as a civil engineer and surveyor, and as this was about the beginning of the era of railway construction there was plenty of work for him in the Old Land, but, like many another youngster, the spirit of adventure had got hold of him, and he was determined to try his fortune in the new world.

In April, 1845, he left Kirkcaldy for Glas-

SANDFORD FLEMING AS A YOUNG MAN AT THE AGE OF THIRTY-THREE. HE WAS THE CHIEF ENGINEER OF THE NORTHERN RAILWAY. IN TWENTY SHORT YEARS HE WAS DESTINED TO WIN UNDYING FAME AS ONE OF THE MASTER BUILDERS OF THE DOMINION.

gow and took passage in a sailing ship to
Quebec. At that time a voyage across the
Atlantic was not such a simple matter as it is
to-day. Sandford Fleming, who was to do
so much to increase and improve the means
of communication, had to be satisfied with
the leisurely speed of an old-fashioned sailing vessel.

It was a fine spring day, the sun high in
the heavens, and the young exile, though his
heart was full, could enjoy the ever-chang-
ing scenery as they glided down the Clyde.
The towers and spires of Glasgow gradually
disappeared in the distance; presently the
traveller passed Dumbarton Castle; the vessel, piloted through such a mass of shipping
as filled him with amazement, dropped down
to Greenock, where a new pilot was taken on
for the Firth of Clyde. "Night comes on
before we reach the Irish sea," says the diary,
"and we go to sleep for the first time on the
deep."

The voyage was comparatively uneventful, and on May 22nd, four weeks after they
left Glasgow, the ship was within sight of
America. "I had just gone on deck," says
Fleming, "when I was greatly surprised to
see hills on the horizon; they had been hid

before by the mist. Every one crowded on deck, some nearly dancing for joy. It was the first I had seen of the new world, the first glimpse of my adopted country."

From Quebec Fleming took a river steamer to Montreal, and from there travelled by another boat up the Ottawa river to Bytown, by way of the Rideau Canal to Kingston, and thence up Lake Ontario to Cobourg. His destination was Peterboro, which he reached by means of a wagon over a rough corduroy road.

Although he made many congenial friends in this picturesque little town, opportunities for work were of course much greater in Toronto, and before the end of August he was settled in the Provincial capital. Fleming was anxious to obtain employment in his own profession, but at that particular time very few public works were in progress, and for some years he had to be content with any work that came to his hand.

He was never idle, however, and in 1849 went down to Montreal to obtain his commission as a provincial land surveyor. While in Montreal he witnessed the burning of the Parliament Buildings by the mob, and he and two or three other men were instrumental in saving the picture of Queen Victoria which hung over the throne and may be seen to-day in the stately Parliament House in Ottawa.

On his return from Montreal he began the practice of his profession, and soon afterward he with several other surveyors, engineers and architects, organized the Canadian Institute, which became the Royal Canadian Institute in 1914, and has been one of the most active agencies in promoting the intellectual and scientific interests of Canada.

In 1853 Fleming began his association with Canadian railways which was to fill so large a part of his life. At that time he joined the staff of the Ontario, Simcoe and Huron Railroad, afterward known as the Northern Railway. He remained for ten years with this company, first as assistant engineer and later as chief engineer. Though comparatively uneventful these were vitally important years to the young engineer. He was passing through the formative period of a man's life, and as the imaginative side found expression in the creation of the Canadian Institute, the practical engineer threw himself heart and soul into the novel problems of a pioneer railway, gaining thereby experience and breadth of vision for the infinitely larger engineering problems that awaited him in the future.

Soon after his settlement in Canada, Fleming began to interest himself in the great question of transportation. He was one of the early advocates of the policy of building a railway across British North America from the Atlantic to the Pacific, and as a preliminary measure suggested the creation of a road from the west end of Lake Superior to the Red River Colony.

In 1863 he was asked, on behalf of the people of the Red River Colony, to present to the Canadian and Imperial Governments a memorial asking for the establishment of means of communication between the eastern provinces and British Columbia by way of the Great Lakes, the Red River country and the Saskatchewan. The idea was that a road might be built from Lake Superior to the Red River, which would afterward be expanded into either a rail and water route or a through railway from ocean to ocean.

This transcontinental railway scheme was one that had already engaged the attention of several far-sighted men, men of big ideas,

men who like Fleming possessed that rare
combination of common sense and imagination that has been the driving force behind
all great public enterprises. The average
man could find in such a project, at such a
time, nothing short of madness; and the
enthusiast who urged it was branded as a
crank.

Because Fleming was a man of big ideas,
with a firm faith in the destiny of his country, he threw himself whole-heartedly into
the project that meant so much to the people
of the Red River Settlement. He urged it
with all his strength upon the then Canadian
Government, and then sailed for England to
lay the scheme before the Imperial Government. Fleming's mission bore no direct
fruit, but there can be no doubt that the seed
was planted which some years afterward
was to grow into Canada's first transcontinental railway.

In 1863 the Governments of Nova Scotia
and New Brunswick, and what was then
known as Canada (the present Provinces of
Ontàrio and Quebec) had decided to carry
out surveys in connection with the proposed
Intercolonial Railway between Quebec and
Halifax. The surveys were to be entrusted

to a Commission of three engineers, one appointed by Canada, the second by Nova Scotia and New Brunswick, and the third by the Imperial Government. It is a tribute to Fleming's growing fame as an engineer, that all these governments nominated the same man and the proposed Commission narrowed down to Sandford Fleming.

This important railway project, with which Fleming was to be associated for some years to come, and whose successful completion was to be mainly due to his ability, energy and determined character, had been under consideration for many years. It is not easy to realize to-day, when one can board a comfortable train at Montreal one afternoon and be in Saint John, New Brunswick, the following morning that in those days a traveller must either take a slow and roundabout route by sea, or an equally roundabout route by land, most of it through foreign territory. Indeed it occupied as much time then to go from Montreal to Halifax as it does to-day to go from Montreal to England.

In estimating the value of Sandford Fleming's services in carrying the Intercolonial through to completion, one must remember what a very important factor that railway was in binding together the then scattered Maritime Provinces and Upper and Lower Canada.

In 1864 there were no roads and no means of communication along the route that was to be surveyed for the Intercolonial. Fleming and his men left Quebec in midwinter and made their way to Rivière du Loup. From thence their surveys had to be made through a region of dense forest. They travelled on snow-shoes and carried their supplies on dog-sleds. Reading between the lines of his diary, jotted down hastily at the end of a hard day's travel, one gets a faint idea of the hardships he had to endure. Some thrifty official at Quebec had provisioned the surveys with canned meat left over from the Crimean War. Many a time the surveyors must have wished that it had been providentially sunk in the Black Sea. Fortunately the country sometimes afforded fish and small game, with an occasional moose to break the monotony of the unpalatable rations of the army contractors.

Finally they reached the little town of Dalhousie, where the night was spent with David Saddler, a surveyor. Saddler had been through the terrible Miramichi fire of 1825, and could still recall the days of horror when whole districts were swept clean of every living thing. For him, however, the fire had not been wholly disastrous. Fortune had enabled him to save from drowning a beautiful young woman, who, with others of her family had fled to the river as a last refuge. In good time she became his wife, and took her place at his own fireside.

From Dalhousie Fleming drove to Bathurst and Newcastle, and then to Fredericton, the capital of New Brunswick. There he was invited by the Governor to dine at Government House. He declined, as he had nothing to wear but his grey homespun suit and red flannel shirt. The Governor, however, insisted that he should come just as he was. "You can imagine," says Fleming, "the sensation I made when I entered the drawing room at Government House, filled with ladies in wonderful toilettes and officers in full dress uniform. However, I was given a charming companion to take in to dinner and enjoyed myself immensely."

Fleming describes a curious incident in connection with one of his survey parties. While at Fredericton he had a visit one morning from a young man who introduced himself as Lord Haddo, and asked to be allowed to join one of the survey parties. Fleming said that it would be impossible to take a traveller or sportsman with the party. "But," said Haddo, "you misunderstand me. I am looking for work, not for game. I want to join your survey, and I can serve as an axeman as well as any other fellow."

Fleming had to return to Quebec, and some time afterward found himself in Halifax, where he was surprised to see Lord Haddo on the dock embarking for Liverpool. He explained that he had just had word of the death of his father, the Earl of Aberdeen, and must return at once to Scotland. "He was," says Fleming, "a man of strong and original views, anxious to feel that he could make his own way in the world apart from the accident of birth, and anxious also to gain first-hand knowledge of the conditions that other men had to face in the new world."

About a year later the young nobleman came out to New Brunswick again, and from there made his way to Gloucester, where he joined the crew of a whaling ship bound for the South Seas. From the day he sailed out of Gloucester Harbour nothing was ever heard of him or of the ship and crew. The Earl of Aberdeen, who some years ago was Governor-General of Canada, was a younger brother of the man who went down in the Gloucester whaler.

Fleming, having completed the surveys for the Intercolonial, was then entrusted with the very important work of building the railway. It was a long, involved and difficult problem, but it was finally carried to a successful completion. In his final report as Chief Engineer Fleming says, "On this day, July 1st, 1876, may be chronicled the completion of the Intercolonial Railway, and the full consummation of the union of the British Provinces in North America." No one but Fleming himself could ever know the whole inner history of the Intercolonial, or how much of his own unconquerable personality went into the work and made possible its successful conclusion. But it is certainly true that the Dominion owes much to this eminent engineer.

While Fleming was still engaged in building the Intercolonial he was offered by the Canadian Government, in 1871, the position of Engineer-in-Chief of the proposed Canadian Pacific Railway. He hesitated to accept the office, feeling, quite naturally, that the responsibilities of the Intercolonial were enough for one man to assume, but he finally consented when the Government put it to him as a matter of public duty.

The situation was extraordinary. The Canadian Pacific Railway, a gigantic undertaking viewed even from the standpoint of to-day, was, in 1871, a project without a parallel in the development of means of transportation. When one places oneself in the Canada of 1871, with its handful of people and its undeveloped resources, it is impossible not to admire the splendid courage of the public men who launched our first transcontinental railway. With such a task to be carried through, it is not to be wondered at that the Government of the day turned to the one Canadian engineer who was big enough to handle such a tremendous problem.

From 1871 to 1880 Sandford Fleming was engaged in directing a series of careful surveys for the line of the Canadian Pacific, and to some extent in building the road. For five years he filled at the same time the positions of Chief Engineer of the Intercolonial and of the Canadian Pacific, and for part of that time he was also Chief Engineer of the Newfoundland Railway. No man, without his extraordinary mental and physical vigour, could have borne the tremendous strain.

The task was herculean. The building of the Intercolonial was itself a work of sufficient magnitude, and it must be remembered that this man put into everything that he undertook a conscientious care that extended to every detail. Yet at the same time he was planning and personally supervising a railway from the Atlantic to the Pacific, the first transcontinental road in North America, and at that time by all odds the most formidable railway project in the world. The work involved surveys through the extremely difficult country north of Lake Superior, among the snow-covered peaks of the Rocky Mountains, and through that veritable sea of mountains that makes up so much of the great Province of British Columbia.

The Canadian Pacific Railway during the period that Fleming was associated with it was a national project. To all intents and purposes it was an extension of the Intercolonial to the Pacific; to link the newly created provinces of Manitoba and British

Columbia to the rest of the Dominion; to create a channel of communication between the east and the west; to open up for settlement the vast fertile plains between Lake Superior and the Rockies. To the Empire it would become a very important link in the chain of communication between the mother country and her far-flung dependencies.

The project appealed to Fleming as a great engineering problem; but even more so as a matter of national and imperial significance. He was then, as always, what might be called a practical Imperialist. He dreamed dreams and formulated projects that were sometimes in advance of his time, but his dreams were never impractical. They looked always to the knitting together of the scattered members of a world-wide empire by creating and improving means of communication; and they had behind them the belief that every advance in the means of communication must inevitably make for better understanding, closer fellowship, and the only lasting form of union among the different branches of the British Empire.

The tremendous difficulties that had to be overcome in building the Canadian Pacific Railway, and even in surveying the route it was to follow, may be realized from the fact that over large portions of the way the surveyors were the first white men to travel. It took a long time to decide how the railway should be carried through the Rockies. There were many passes, and each of them had to be carefully surveyed to find which would be most favourable for the purposes of the railway. Fleming's final conclusion was that the Yellowhead Pass offered the best possible route, because of the fact that the line could be carried through it without any heavy grades. For political or other reasons his recommendations were not accepted, and the Canadian Pacific was finally built through the Kicking Horse Pass, which involved very much steeper grades than the Yellowhead, and added enormously to the cost, both of construction and operation. Fleming's judgment was justified many years afterward when both the Grand Trunk Pacific and the Canadian Northern were carried through the Yellowhead Pass into British Columbia.

In 1872 Fleming, having carefully examined the reports of his engineers, thought it wise to study with his own eyes the main features of the route that had then been selected for the Canadian Pacific Railway. The story of this important journey was afterwards told by George Munro Grant, his companion on the trip, in a book entitled *Ocean to Ocean.*

From Prince Arthur's Landing on Lake Superior, later known as Port Arthur, the party followed the Dawson Route, by wagon and canoe, to Fort Garry, now Winnipeg. Here saddle-horses were procured, with Red River carts for the baggage, and they set out over the great plains for the mountains, travelling by way of Fort Ellice, Fort Carlton and Fort Edmonton, posts of the Hudson's Bay Company. On the way they met or passed numbers of hunting or trading parties, traders going west and the Métis returning east with carts well laden with buffalo skins and dried meat.

"A number of Red River people club together in the spring and go west to hunt the buffalo. Their caravan is popularly called a 'brigade' and very picturesque is its appearance on the road or around the camp-fire. The old men, the women, and little children are engaged on the expedition, and all help. The men ride and the women drive the carts. The children make the fires and do chores. The men shoot buffalo; the women dry the meat and make it into pemmican."

From Edmonton the route lay over the Rocky Mountains by way of Yellowhead Pass. Fresh saddle-horses were obtained from the Hudson's Bay Company, and the carts were abandoned for pack-horses accustomed to the peculiarities of mountain trails.

At one of the camps, on the banks of the Athabasca, a curious relic of early days came to light.

"While hacking with his axe at the brush on the camping-ground, just where our heads would lie, Brown struck something metallic that blunted the edge of the axe. Feeling with his hand he drew out from near the root of a young spruce tree an ancient sword bayonet, the brazen hilt and steel blade in excellent preservation, but the leather scabbard half eaten as if by the teeth of some animal. It seemed strange in this vast and silent forest wilderness thus to come upon a relic that told, probably, of the old days when the two rival fur companies armed their agents to the teeth, and when bloody contests often took place between them."

The old sword in its rotting scabbard hung for years on the walls of Fleming's home in Ottawa, among other mementoes of the far west.

Making their way into the mountains and up to the extraordinarily low summit of

Yellowhead Pass, Fleming and his companions entered British Columbia, and after a rather strenuous journey down the valley of the North Thompson River arrived at Kamloops about the end of September. Here they encountered one of the characteristic supply-trains on its way up to Tête Jaune Cache—fifty-two mules led by a bell-horse and driven by four or five men representing as many different nationalities.

From Kamloops Fleming had a comparatively easy journey down to Lytton, at the junction of the Thompson and the Fraser, thence to Yale by the famous road, hewn in places out of the face of the rock hundreds of feet above the bed of the river; and from Yale down the river by steamer to New Westminster. A pleasant sail through the Straits of Georgia, with a brief visit to Bute Inlet, brought the travellers to Vancouver Island and the pretty little town of Victoria, something over three months from the day they had left Halifax.

In 1883 Fleming again travelled across the continent, this time crossing the Rockies by way of the Kicking Horse Pass. He describes the journey in his book *Old and New Westminster*. One is struck with the change in the means of transportation that had taken place in eleven years. The first journey on horseback occupied thirty-six days, from Fort Garry to the mountains; the second journey by rail was made in fifty-six hours.

A good deal of anxiety was felt at this time as to the possibility of getting the railway through the mountains. The Kicking Horse Pass route had been explored, and it was known that it was practicable, although difficult, as far as the valley of the Columbia. Nothing was yet known, however, as to the next range of mountains, the Selkirks. To Fleming's immense relief he met Major Rogers, who had been exploring in the Selkirks, and learned that a pass had been found by way of the Beaver River and the Illecillewaet. That would bring them to the second crossing of the Columbia, and it was already known that the railway could be built through the Gold Range by way of Eagle Pass.

Without attempting to follow Fleming on his eventful journey through the mountains to the coast, one passage in his book may be quoted, to give some idea of the hard work that was involved in surveying a route for the Canadian Pacific Railway. Fleming is speaking of the journey through the Selkirks.

"The walking is dreadful; we climb over and creep under fallen trees of great size, and the men soon show that they feel the weight of their burdens. Their halts for rest are frequent. It is hot work for us all. The dripping rain from the bush and branches saturate us from above. Tall ferns sometimes reaching to the shoulder, and devil's clubs through which we have to crush our way, make us feel as if dragged through a horse-pond, and our perspiration is that of a Turkish bath. We meet with obstacles of every description. The devil's clubs may be numbered by millions, and they are perpetually wounding us with their spikes against which we strike. We halt very frequently for rest. Our advance is varied by ascending rocky slopes and slippery masses, and again descending to a lower level. We wade through alder swamps and tread down skunk cabbage and the prickly aralias, and so we continue until half-past four, when the tired-out men are unable to go farther. A halt becomes necessary. We camp for the night on a high bank overlooking the Illecillewaet. Our advance on a direct line we estimate at four miles!"

Two years later a dramatic incident took place in the history of Canada's first transcontinental railway—the driving of the last spike. Fleming was one of the chief actors in this historic episode, and tells the story. There was nothing very romantic in the actual scene—a group of railway men and in their midst three notable Canadians, Donald Smith (afterwards Lord Strathcona), Sandford Fleming and William Van Horne. The surroundings were not at all inspiring; a cutting slashed through the forest and down the centre of it two lines of steel, a desolate array of stumps and a sea of mud, a crowd of uninteresting-looking men, mostly unshaven, and in the foreground an elderly gentleman driving a spike.

But what a story lay behind the driving of that iron spike! The story of a young country inspired by the splendid optimism of youth! The story of an imperial dream and what came of it! A land of magnificent distances and incalculable resources, with a sparse population and very little capital. What madness to assume the burden of a transcontinental railway!

Shrewd onlookers shook their wise heads and warned that the railway would not earn enough to pay for its axle-grease!

This little group standing in the mud at

Craigellachie, in Eagle Pass, around an iron spike, saw the completion of the transcontinental railway. One part of their dream had come true. The other—the splendid success of the daring experiment—has long since been proved beyond all possible dispute. Not the least important of the actors in this national drama was Sandford Fleming.

So far Fleming has been considered as a man who planned and built great railways. He may now be introduced in another but equally important rôle. Probably none of the great projects associated with Fleming's name more strikingly illustrates his sheer tenacity of purpose—quiet, unostentatious, almost apologetic, but none the less compelling—than the movement for a British, state-owned cable across the Pacific. From 1879, when he first broached the subject, to 1902, when the cable was actually laid from Vancouver Island to New Zealand and Australia, he kept the matter alive not only in Canada but in England and Australasia; kept it alive and moving, though the forces arrayed against him, open and hidden, were enough to have daunted even a man of so strong and untiring a purpose.

It was, indeed, a long and uphill fight against tremendous odds. Fleming had to overcome first of all the apathy of the people of Canada and the other self-governing colonies; then the inactivity of the British Government; finally the powerful opposition of the group of wealthy cable companies which held a monopoly of the business between England and Australia, and, naturally enough, were loath to part with it. Nevertheless, patience and perseverance won the day, as they generally do when enlisted in a good cause, and backed by brains. The Pacific Cable has been in operation now for many years, and it would be difficult to overestimate its value as a means of bringing closer together the scattered members of the British Empire.

But Sandford Fleming was never contented with a bite while the rest of the apple was in sight. Having secured the Pacific Cable, he immediately started an active agitation for its logical development, a system of submarine cables and land telegraphs circling the globe, touching only British territory, and owned by the Empire. This he called the All-Red Line. Up to the time of his death, Fleming was still pressing this important scheme upon the attention of governments and public organizations throughout the Empire. He did not live to see it carried out, nor is it yet an accomplished fact, but progress has been made, and in course of time the British Empire will enjoy the fruits of Sandford Fleming's far-sighted and patriotic dream.

We have grown so used to the system of Standard Time, that is the division of the earth into zones within which all have the same time, that we hardly realize the inconvenience of the old system, or lack of system, that was used a few years ago. In Fleming's day, for instance, no less than five different standards of time were used between Halifax and Toronto. To-day there are only four changes between the Atlantic and the Pacific, and they are at fixed points. Here, again, the people of Canada and other countries have to thank Sandford Fleming for patiently persuading them to drop the old, cumbersome and very inconvenient way of measuring time in favour of a uniform system. It seems incredible that it should have taken years to secure the adoption of this sensible reform, but people are very loath to abandon clumsy expedients to which they have grown accustomed.

One may fittingly sum up the life of Sandford Fleming in his own words.

"I have often thought how grateful I am for my birth into this marvellous world, and how anxious I have always been to justify it. I have dreamed my little dreams, I have planned my little plans, and begrudged no effort to bring about what I regarded as desirable results. I have always felt that the humblest among us has it in his power to do something for his country by doing his duty, and that there is no better inheritance to leave his children than the knowledge that he has done so to the utmost of his ability.

"It has been my great good fortune to have had my lot cast in this goodly land, and to have been associated with its educational and material prosperity. Nobody can deprive me of the satisfaction I feel in having had the opportunity and the will to strive for the advancement of Canada and the good of the empire. I am profoundly thankful for length of days, for active, happy years, for friendships formed, and especially for the memory of those dear souls who have enriched my own life while they remained on this side."

LORD STRATHCONA

by

Howard Angus Kennedy

LORD STRATHCONA

EDWARD the Seventh, King and Emperor, called him "Dear Uncle Donald." To us, the rank and file of common citizens, especially in Canada but also in the mother-land, he was a sort of fairy godfather. At one touch of his magic wand, a regiment of cavalry sprang up from the plain; another touch, and a college for women rose on the mountain side. One touch would banish care from a single troubled heart, the next would heal a multitude. That golden wand was busy all the time. He loved to use it.

No fairy godfather came to his own aid, when he was a boy on the banks of a Scottish stream, or even when he reached this land of hope and opportunity. Witches, rather than fairies, seemed to follow him from the "blasted heath." It was there that Shakespeare's three hags met Macbeth on his fateful way to Forres—the town where Donald Alexander Smith was born in 1820. If he himself had met three witches, or three hundred, he would have snapped his fingers at them. The disappointments of his early life never made him bitter, or cynical. He just went on serenely through them all, and made the best of things.

He made the best of his schooling, for one thing. In both mathematics and classics he distinguished himself.

When he left school, he had no fixed programme of life. For a while he just drifted. He got a job in the Town Clerk's office, and learned to keep accounts. He studied a little law. His mother's cousins, two mercantile brothers named Grant, offered him a desk in their office at Manchester. They were a delightful pair. Read Dickens's "Nicholas Nickleby," if you would like to meet them—they were his Cheeryble Brothers, the models of genial generosity.

A more adventurous life filled Donald's dreams, than clerking even for Cheerybles. Sitting at a desk and scratching paper is a poor, unnatural occupation for a healthy natural man. Donald was that sort of man, or boy, and in his eighteenth year he set off for Canada. He walked all the way to Aberdeen, embarked in a coasting schooner for London, there took passage in another sailing

LORD STRATHCONA AND MOUNT ROYAL, FORMERLY DONALD A. SMITH, ONE OF THE MASTER BUILDERS OF CANADA, WAS GOVERNOR OF THE HUDSON'S BAY COMPANY, 1889-1914, AND HIGH COMMISSIONER FOR CANADA, IN LONDON, ENGLAND, 1896-1914.

ship, and landed at Quebec after a six weeks' voyage.

Donald had thought of settling in Ontario, then known as Upper Canada. But an uncle, an old fur-trader in the Hudson's Bay Company, had given him a letter of introduction to Sir George Simpson, Governor of that great corporation. Sir George held his court at Lachine, above the rapids from Montreal. There they met—the little autocrat, ruler of all the land we know as Canada to-day except the south-east corner, and the tall fair-haired youth destined fifty years later to inherit his throne and the remains of his kingdom.

"Take him to the fur room," the Governor called to a clerk, "and teach him to count rats."

So, counting muskrat skins and beaver and fox and the rest pouring in from the wilderness, Donald Smith made his humble entry to the Company's service. He never left it. He was a Hudson's Bay man, though so much else, for three-quarters of a century.

He counted those skins right, you may be sure. He could not bear to be inaccurate, in figures or in words. He learned not only to count but to judge and value every kind of fur; and he had to check the accounts coming in from all the Company's hundred and fifty posts between Labrador and Vancouver Island.

Then in 1841, after a three years' apprenticeship, the time came for his first step up the ladder, his plunge into the wilderness where all the serious climbing had to be done.

Not being a favourite of the Governor's, he had no chance of appointment to one of the coveted posts in the farthest west. He was sent east instead, and spent seven years among posts on the north shore of the Lower St. Lawrence. There you can imagine him, travelling about among poor thriftless Montagnais Indians, keeping them in good humour as he bargained for their furs; among the scattered French-Canadians too, perfecting himself in their language and learning their ways of thought.

The kindly and courtly white-bearded old gentleman that we knew so well—we must picture him to ourselves as a stalwart youth in red flannel shirt and rough grey homespun trousers, shod in deerskin moccasins, his long fair hair escaping from a coloured woollen tuque. Out on the winter trail we see him striding along on his snowshoes, with hunting knife and gun, a dog sled carrying his blankets, grub and kettle. At home in one or other of the posts, there were the Company's accounts to be kept, visiting trappers to be entertained and bargained with. In his spare time there were letters to be written, especially to the dear old mother over the sea; and in reading books he found endless pleasure. People who seldom read a book have no idea what a wonderful delight they miss.

His eyes, however, troubled him. They grew more and more painful, till he feared he would go blind. He wrote the Governor for leave to come up and seek medical advice. No answer came. He wrote again, and yet again. Still no answer. Delay might be dangerous, and he set off without leave, for the Company's headquarters at Lachine. Sir George asked his doctor to examine the young man. The doctor prescribed the necessary treatment, but said there was no fear of blindness.

"This appears to me a serious case of indiscipline," the angry Governor said. "It is now eight o'clock. I will give you thirty minutes to leave for your new post!" He was banished to the wilderness of Eastern Labrador.

On the point of rebellion, Donald controlled himself and went.

It was a terrible journey, in midwinter and afoot, from Quebec to Mingan and the North. He and his two Indian guides lost their way in a snowstorm. Game was scarce, and they nearly starved. One of the Indians died. Exhausted, and suffering acutely with his eyes, the young man reached Masquarro. There the Company's agent kept him till spring, with the good excuse that no Indian guides could be found before.

When Donald Smith reached his final destination, he was agreeably disappointed. The North-west River Post looked out on Esquimaux Bay, or Hamilton Inlet, a salt-water lake connecting with the Atlantic sixty miles farther east. It was a beautiful and sheltered spot, well wooded, and quite unlike the bleak sea-coast that gave Labrador its name of barren desolation. Berries there were in plenty, as well as trees; caribou and black bear for meat, with wild goose, duck and partridge; salmon in summer and trout the year round. "We can if we choose," Donald wrote home, "make our tea of the Labrador tea plant."

If nature unhelped could be so generous, he thought, what might she do with a little help from science and industry?

The Moravian missionaries had not only half converted the Nascopie Indians of that region—at one point they had made a little farm. Donald Smith followed their example and bettered it. He became Chief Trader in 1852, and one of his first acts of authority was to create a model farm.

He brought sheep and horses round by sea from Canada. He imported cattle, poultry, and seeds of hardy vegetables, from the Orkneys, a group of Scottish islands famous in our country's annals as a rich recruiting ground for the Hudson's Bay ranks. He ploughed the land and fertilized it with fish offal. He built the first road, and drove the first wheeled vehicle ever seen in Labrador.

"The astonished ear" of a scientist from Washington, arriving to watch an eclipse of the sun, was greeted, he tells us, with the lowing of cattle, the bleating of sheep, and "cackle ominous of new-laid eggs." The fragrance of new-mown hay in the barn, of flowers in the garden—melons and cucumbers, potatoes and turnips, peas, pumpkins and cauliflower, barley and oats—a bull and twelve cows, sheep, goats, chickens—a team of horses trotting down a two-mile carriage road—what could it mean?

"Surely," the visitor exclaims, "nature has been remarkably lavish here, or some presiding genius, of no ordinary enterprise and taste, has redeemed the place from its wilderness desolation . . Both are true. Donald Alexander Smith, the intelligent agent, is a practical farmer, and succeeds in forcing to maturity most of the vegetables and grains produced in warmer latitudes. He has seven acres under cultivation, a considerable portion under glass.

"There is no other place like Smith's in Labrador, in all its area of 420,000 square miles."

After the American astronomer, came the famous British Arctic explorer, Sir Leopold McClintock. He was surveying the coast to find the best landing place for a transatlantic telegraph cable.

Amazed at the miracle of Esquimaux Bay, he gives this picture of the fur-trading farmer who had worked it:

"About 40 years old, some five feet ten high, with long sandy hair, a bushy red beard, and very thick red eyebrows. He was dressed in a black swallow-tail coat, not at all according to the fashion of the country, and wore a white linen shirt"—just to honour the guest, no doubt. "Although his countenance could hardly be called handsome, it was distinguished, and his manners were irreproachable. His talk showed him to be a man of superior intelligence."

"I see, Mr. Smith," said the captain, "you're not a man to be content with conditions as you find them in this world."

"Who would be?" Smith replied. "The world would be a very sad place if we couldn't make it a little better!"

As the captain went back to his ship, he remarked to a brother officer—"Labrador won't hold this man!"

The fur-trader's chief object in creating the farm was to keep his men in better health and comfort with fresh vegetables, milk and eggs. He could hardly persuade them at first to plough or dig, but by-and-by every man had his own patch of root crops, and it made a great difference in their lives.

He watched over them like a father. He was not merely their "boss," but their doctor, minister, and judge. A busy man indeed was Donald Smith. He had to manage the buying, packing and shipping of fish as well as fur. Salmon was exported in large quantities to London and Montreal. He even established a salmon cannery.

His reading now had a double object— both to furnish and entertain his own mind, and to increase his efficiency as farmer, gardener, stockraiser, and in all his other capacities as sole chief of an isolated community. The post had a little library, and he added to it, choosing his books with his usual care. He studied medicine, botany and zoology, as well as history, philosophy, theology and political economy.

In after years he would smile when people asked if he had not suffered terribly from the boredom, the *ennui*, of his twenty years' exile in that wilderness. "I assure you," said he, "there was no such thing as *ennui* in Labrador!"

A busy man, and therefore a happy one. Hard work was good for him, as it is for us all. He made duty his master, and found it his friend.

Another rich source of happiness he discovered in Labrador. There it was he met and married Isabella, daughter of Richard Hardisty, Chief Trader before him in charge of North-west River. It was a very happy marriage. Donald and Isabella were lovers to the end—for more than sixty years.

A quarter of a century had passed since Donald Smith made his home in Canada when he again crossed the sea on his first visit to the old home and mother in Scotland. Then, returning to Labrador, he took up contentedly the threads of his varied life on the beautiful bay. But events outside were moving fast, and it was his destiny to take a leading part in shaping them. It was well for the country that in 1868 he was called away from his secluded nook to the Canadian metropolis, though at the time he thought he was only going on his Company's business, to manage its Montreal Department. He took up his new duty, and indeed became General Manager of all the Company's business in the East.

It was a cry of distress from the West, however, and not big business in the East, that brought him swiftly to the front.

That vast empty land—for a dozen years Canadians had been thinking much about its future. The Hudson's Bay Company had held and governed it for nigh two hundred years, under a charter given by King Charles II. To the Company, it was just a game preserve, a profitable source of fur supply.

Explorers sent out by Canada in 1857, however, had reported enormous areas of the West as naturally fitted for cultivation. When the Canadian Provinces federated, ten years later, the new Dominion Government set itself to acquire the West for this purpose. The Company's shareholders in England agreed to surrender their charter to the Imperial Government, which was then to hand over the Territory to Canada. The Dominion Government agreed to pay the Company $1,500,000 cash, and to leave it in possession of its trading posts and much land besides; also, to protect the rights of the Indians and those of the Métis in the Territory.

The Métis, restless at this turn of events, now decided to take matters into their own hands. They did not know, in fact the Canadian authorities had not yet decided, exactly what form of government they would have to obey. They feared they might be worse off under the new rulers than under the old. At any rate, they had not been consulted about the change.

Some of the Métis, with Louis Riel at their head, seized the Hudson's Bay headquarters at Fort Garry, in the Red River Settlement. They would not even let the new Governor enter the Territory. He had come round from Ottawa through the United States, and they stopped him on the frontier at Pembina.

Now the Hudson's Bay officers had not been consulted either, when the Company gave up its charter. They were partners in the Company's business, and they were not satisfied with the terms of the agreement made by the shareholders in England. False reports were spread, therefore, that some of them were encouraging the Métis revolt.

Sir John Macdonald, the Canadian Prime Minister, sent for Donald Smith as the Company's head man in the East. Mr. Smith declared himself a staunch Canadian. He favoured the transfer of the West to Canada, and before the Imperial Government would make that transfer the trouble on the Red River would have to be settled. "If there is no transfer of the Territory," he said, "law and order and property will be at the mercy of the most lawless members of the community—until the Americans step in and annex it,"—as some hotheads were openly planning to do.

Sir John promptly asked him to go West as a Special Commissioner of the Government and try to smooth matters over. Donald Smith agreed, and hurried off accordingly.

A threatening letter was put into his hands as he passed through St. Paul. The nameless writer warned him solemnly to go no farther. "Pause now before it is too late. Your blood be upon your own head!"

But he knew well the risk he was taking, and went to face it. At Fort Garry he was made a prisoner. Riel would not let him either leave the fort or receive visitors within it. His brother-in-law, Richard Hardisty, however, went about among the Métis, and got many of them to promise their support. Riel at last agreed that the people of the settlement should be allowed to hear what the Commissioner had to say, and a public meeting was called for the nineteenth of January.

It was a bitterly cold day, twenty below zero with a cutting wind, when Riel and Smith stepped on to a platform in the fort enclosure and faced the crowd. Many of the Métis were armed. The Commissioner was constantly interrupted, he was even threatened with death, but he succeeded in reading aloud the Governor-General's assurance of fair treatment for all the people.

Even a message from Queen Victoria was interrupted by the angry Métis, as the Commissioner went on to read it. Her Majesty said that she viewed with sorrow and displeasure the unreasonable and lawless proceedings which had taken place. If the people addressed to her representative, the Governor-General, their desires or complaints, he would always receive them; but he would also suppress unlawful disturbances.

The people were calmed by the fairness of these assurances. A Convention was elected, half English and half French-speaking. It drew up a list of "rights," and sent off three delegates to discuss these with the Government at Ottawa.

Riel, however, also got the Convention to approve of a "Provisional Government," he himself being the "President." He was angered because the Convention had disagreed with some of his proposals, and furious when an armed party from Portage la Prairie arrived in the settlement to demand the release of his loyalist prisoners.

The prisoners were set free—but when the Portage men started for home a large number of them were made prisoners instead. Riel was on the point of shooting their leader, Captain Boulton, and only spared his life at Donald Smith's urgent request. Another prisoner, Thomas Scott, being particularly outspoken, was sentenced to death. On the fourth of March he was shot.

Disgusted with the affair, the Commissioner would have nothing more to do with Riel, except to demand freedom to depart.

He had now done all he could—and that
was much. With great tact and force he
had dispelled many fears and suspicions
among the people, and paved the way for a
final settlement. With much difficulty, and
after a fortnight's delay, he secured his
liberty and made his way back to Canada.

With Colonel Wolseley's expedition to
restore order and establish the new Province
of Manitoba, the Commissioner reached
Fort Garry once more in the following
August. Riel fled, and Donald Smith presided over the infant province until its
Lieutenant-Governor arrived.

If the Hudson's Bay man thought this
would set him free to attend to his Company's business, he soon found he was mis-
taken. He was not ambitious for public life,
and too independent in mind to make an
obedient party politician. But the people of
Winnipeg insisted on making him their representative in the first Legislature of the
province, and a few months later he was also
elected member for Selkirk in the Federal
House of Commons—a double honour since
forbidden by the law.

With heart and soul, and head besides, he

threw himself into his new work—to develop the West, its resources, its population, its prosperity.

From the very start, he saw that not much progress could be hoped for till East and West were joined by a chain of steel rails.

In his first public speech at Ottawa, in 1871, he contradicted the idea that the building of such a railway would be too difficult. He believed the line would be built within ten years.

He would only have laughed if some prophetic soul had answered, "In ten years you'll be building it yourself, Donald!"

He had been thrifty, like most of his brother Scots. He had made a habit of saving half his pay, even when the whole of it was only $100 a year. But he was not rich, still less did he seem on the road to become a millionaire. Even if he had been, he thought a transcontinental railway could only be built by the resources of a Government.

Well, the Government tried, and failed.

It is true that Sir Hugh Allan, the steamship magnate and then the richest man in Canada, proposed to build the line by means of a company largely financed by capitalists in the United States. Sir John Macdonald's Government promised to help with a grant of $30,000,000 from the country's pocket and 50,000,000 acres of public land. That scheme, however, came to grief on the discovery that Sir John and his colleagues had privately accepted large sums from Sir Hugh and his friends, to help the Government party in winning a general election.

A storm broke out when this "Pacific Scandal" came to light. The Government tried to defend itself in the House of Commons, but could not depend on its usual majority. Donald Smith was reckoned a supporter of the Government, but he declared with great regret that he could not conscientiously vote for it under such circumstances.

That was enough. The Government took the warning, and resigned before the House could come to a vote. Sir John from that day was Donald Smith's enemy. It was years before they were even outwardly reconciled.

Another Highland Scot, Alexander Mackenzie, the working stonemason who had risen to lead the Opposition in the Parliament of Canada, now became Prime Minister, and a general election gave him a majority.   He set aside the scheme of an all-rail route across the Dominion.   The West would have to be content, for a time, with a combined land-and-water route.   The Government would build sections of railway from the head of the great lakes to Lake of the Woods, from Lake of the Woods to the prairies, and by degrees, in fulfilment of a solemn pledge long before given to British Columbia, across the mountains to the Pacific.

The only railway communication between Eastern and Western Canada would still be through the States and beyond Canada's own control—by way of St. Paul.   In winter, with lake navigation stopped, this would be the only steam route of any kind.

And even this route was not yet available. A company in the United States had started to build a line up through Minnesota to the British frontier at Pembina, but had failed. Passengers and freight had still to be carried by trail, or in summer by the Red River, between Fort Garry and the head of steel in the United States.

Donald Smith, of course, as a Hudson's Bay man, knew this old route well. The Hudson's Bay Company had put a steamer on the Red River. The Company's agent at St. Paul had latterly been carrying on this navigation in partnership with James J. Hill, a Canadian long settled in Minnesota. Smith and Hill in 1876 laid their heads together to see if the bankrupt railway could not be bought and finished to Pembina. From that frontier point the Canadian Government planned to build a line north to Winnipeg, and an all-rail connection of sorts between Eastern and Western Canada would be complete. But where was the money to come from? Smith and Hill had not got it.

Just then George Stephen and R. B. Angus, President and General Manager of the Bank of Montreal, were compelled to visit Chicago on business. The business was put off for a week. How should they spend the time? One proposed a trip to St. Paul, the other to St. Louis. They tossed a coin to decide.

St. Paul won. There they met Smith and Hill, and listened to their great railway scheme. They went over the rusty track of the unfinished line. By finishing it, they could not only give Western Canada railway connection with the outside world but secure a land grant of several million acres in Minnesota.

The land was just then a drug in the market. It was overrun by a grasshoppers, and settlers were slow to comé in. But that could not last. The Canadians saw their opportunity, and seized it. With the Bank of Montreal's help they bought the line cheap, and finished it. The grasshoppers died out, the farmers poured in, the land was snapped up, and traffic receipts grew fast.

Donald Smith had become a millionaire. So had Stephen, Angus and Hill. What should they do with their millions?

Another failure gave them another opportunity. This time it was the Dominion Government's failure to finish the transcontinental railway in ten years as promised to British Columbia in 1871. True, there were three years still to run when the Mackenzie Government's defeat in 1878 brought Sir

John back to power; but only a few hundred miles of line had yet been put in hand. The railway could not possibly be finished in the promised time.

All the more reason, then, for getting it done as soon as possible.

Railway building by Government was given up as hopeless. A company must be formed to do it after all. Stephen, appealed to by Sir John, gathered a group of his friends together, and they agreed to do the work, with a grant of $25,000,000 and 25,-000,000 acres from the Government. They formed the Canadian Pacific Railway Company, and started operations in May of 1881.

Curiously enough, Donald Smith's name did not appear in any public list of the men interested in the scheme. The Prime Minister had never forgiven him for his fatal speech on the Pacific Scandal, and Smith was content to keep out of sight while his friends discussed terms with the Government. He had privately agreed, all the same, to do his utmost for the success of Sir John's great scheme.

He knew the task would be tremendously hard. It proved far more costly than he had imagined, but he never weakened. More than once the Company found it could not pay its most pressing debts. Both Stephen and Smith pawned nearly everything they had to carry on the work.

Even that was not enough, and bankruptcy loomed ahead. Their own fortunes would have gone down in the wreck, and they were no longer young men to start afresh in life.

"Gentlemen," said President Stephen at one meeting of the directors, "it looks as if we had to burst."

"It may be that we must succumb," said Donald Smith, "but not as long as we individually have a dollar."

It took tremendous bursts of energy to fight, simultaneously, the forces of finance, politics, and an unwilling nature in order to bridge the nation with bands of steel. In the end they triumphed! The railway was completed, the nation was united!

On the 7th of November, 1885, not ten years but less than five from the turning of the first sod, the last spike was driven at Craigellachie, a lonely spot in British

Columbia, on the western slope of the Selkirk Range. The chain of steel was complete, stretching in one unbroken line from ocean to ocean.

Donald Smith was chosen to drive that last spike. As Sir Charles Tupper afterwards said, "The Canadian Pacific Railway would have no existence to-day, notwithstanding all the Government did to support that undertaking, had it not been for the indomitable pluck and energy and determination, both financially and in every other respect, of Sir Donald Smith."

He received his knighthood, and George Stephen was made a baronet, when the line was declared ready for official opening in 1886. These men had done a great thing, not only for Canada but for all our British brotherhood of nations. Queen Victoria herself, telegraphing her congratulations to Canada on the completion of the line, declared it to be "of great importance to the whole British Empire."

That great fight won, did the victor retire, to live at ease and spend his money at his pleasure? Not for a moment!

Like a youngster he cheerfully started on

a fresh career when most men would call themselves aged. He was nearly seventy-six when the Canadian Government asked him to represent the Dominion as "High Commissioner" in London. From that time until a few days before his death at ninety-three, as our national spokesman and business manager at the imperial capital, he led a life of most strenuous and useful hard work. Everything he could do to uphold the honour and advance the prosperity of Canada, he did, with a youthful zest and wise activity as great as the keenest business man could ever devote to his private affairs.

Two meals a day, and eleven hours of work in between—how many business men would keep that up, or even try? Generally the long day was spent at his desk. That alone would be irksome enough for any man used to the open-air life. When he did get out, it was not for recreation. Then, and in the evening when he might be resting in his slippers, he was always ready to take part in some public gathering, if he could say a good word for Canada.

To encourage good people over there to come and make new homes among us—that,

he clearly saw, was the most pressing of all
Canada's needs, as it is more than ever to-
day.   He spent his strength unstintedly, and
took constant delight, in telling the world of
our unrivalled opportunities for the industrious home-maker.

"I don't care what they say of myself," he
wrote, "but they must not abuse Canada
while I am alive to defend her!"

"We have upon the whole," he declared,
"the best climate in the world," and he had
often had his fill of the worst of it.   He
liked the winter best.   "The exhilarating
atmosphere makes for health and every sort
of alertness," he said—alertness of body and
of mind.   "Northern people have always
stood for courage and unconquerability.
They have the muscle, the wholesomeness of
life and the *will*."

It amazed the easy-going stay-at-homes,
and often alarmed his friends, his habit of
dashing off across the Atlantic, not to speak
of remote parts of the British Isles, when the
interests of Canada called him.   One summer, I remember, when he was nearly ninety,
finding him unexpectedly at his desk in
London when he was supposed to be

taking a holiday in Glencoe, his beloved Highland home. It was the second time in a few weeks he had torn himself away and made that six-hundred-mile dash to attend to Canadian business in London.

"Do you enjoy railway travelling?" I asked.—"No, I can't say I do."

"Then I hope you enjoy the sea, for you cross it often enough?"

"No," said he, smiling, "I don't. But when I feel it my duty to go, I just go!"

Like all true Scots, he knew how wonderfully their national love of education and reading had increased both their own success and happiness and their usefulness to the community. He gave millions to bring a high degree of education within the reach of others. His gifts to McGill University in Montreal amounted to more than $2,000,000, besides half a million given by his generous wife and daughter. He spent a million to create the Royal Victoria College for women close by, and sent it another $45,000 every year. To Queen's University at Kingston he gave $100,000; to Yale, over the border, half a million; to Aberdeen University, over the sea, $175,000. Both McGill and Aberdeen elected him Chancellor. He was made a peer of the United Kingdom in 1896, and by special permission the peerage was allowed to pass to his daughter. He had no son.

When the South African War broke out in 1899, he added to the Canadian forces fighting for the Empire a whole regiment of cavalry—"Strathcona's Horse." It cost him a million dollars to equip and carry oversea those four hundred hardy Westerners, and at the close of their engagement he presented the Imperial Government with all their horses and equipment. A few years later he gave the Canadian Government $250,000 to encourage physical and military training in our schools. He was no warlike "militarist," but, as he said, "the first duty of a free citizen is to be prepared to defend his country."

On the slopes of Mount Royal, he and his cousin George Stephen built and equipped the Royal Victoria Hospital. It cost them $1,000,000, besides $800,000 for endowment, and when the building was damaged by fire Donald Smith sent $250,000 for repairs. In England, he gave a million to King Edward's Fund for the London Hospitals, and $52,500 to Queen Alexandra's Fund for the unemployed.

These were only his larger gifts, which came to the ears of the public. We who knew him in private, admired and loved him still more for his unbounded generosity in thousands of cases which the public never heard of. And he seemed to take a personal interest in the people he helped, even when he knew nothing of them beyond what they told him. His charity came warm from the heart.

One Christmas Day he had asked Dr. Grenfell to come to Hudson's Bay House and talk over the needs of the doctor's mission of mercy to the Labrador fisherfolk. Donald Smith had been Governor of the Hudson's Bay Company since 1889. When the visitor rang, it was the aged High Commissioner himself who opened the door. Every one else was taking holiday.

"When we went in," the doctor says, "he was opening letters from an almost endless pile. 'These are all requests for help,' he said. 'I like to deal with them personally when I get time.   But I have calculated that if I granted them all I shouldn't have a single cent left.' "

He was happily spared the world's Great War.   On the 21st of January, 1914, only ten weeks after his wife had been taken, he followed her.   Almost hand in hand, they entered God's Great Peace.

Queen Alexandra spoke truth when she called him "one of the Empire's kindest of men and the greatest of benefactors."

We do not admire him for his money. We honour him for using so much of it so well, and, chiefly, for not being spoilt by its possession.   He was a patriot: for us he freely spent himself, a far greater deed than his spending of money upon us.

To our Hall of Heroes, no money can buy entrance. We remember with pride that Donald Smith, long years before his money came, had earned a place in that brave company.